AGAINST THE ODDS

HOW AN 18-YEAR-OLD KID MADE $2 MILLION DOLLARS IN ONE YEAR

SHUBHAM KUMAR

AGAINST THE ODDS

by
Shubham Kumar

Published by
Authority on Demand

ISBN-13: 978-1545046791
ISBN-10: 1545046794

No part of this book may be reproduced or utilized in
any form or by any means, electronic or mechanical including photocopying, recording, or by any information storage and retrieval system, without permission in writing from the publishers.

© 2017 **Shubham Kumar**

I dedicate this book, with deep respect and great love, to my parents. You gave me not only the gift of life but also an unrelenting passion to live it fully. For that, I am so very grateful.

CONTENTS

PROLOGUE	**7**
CHAPTER 1:	**15**
HOW IT ALL STARTED	15
WHAT IS MY AIM?	18
ENGINEERING MANIA	21
TRAIN TO PATNA	24
WAS IT AN ILLUSION?	32
LIFE-CHANGING DECISION	35
CHAPTER 2:	**41**
SAY 'NO' SO YOUR 'YESES' HAVE MORE OOMPH	41
CHALLENGE ACCEPTED	48
DEAL WITH NEGATIVITY POSITIVELY	63
MY FIRST LOVE IS MY FIRST SALE OF $220	71
CHAPTER 3:	**81**
BEGINNING OF A NEW ERA	81
ON-THE-JOB TRAINING	87

DEALING WITH RIGHT PERSON AND WRONG PERSON	96
UNEXPECTED SHIT HAPPENS	106
FINALLY, WE GOT STARTED FOR REAL	117
CHAPTER 4:	**121**
STEP IN ONLINE BUYING-SELLING WORLD	121
E-COMMERCE TALKS	128
YO! GOT A POTENTIAL MARKET	135
CHAPTER 5:	**139**
FROM GRIEF TO GLORY	139
ADVERSITY LED DIVERSITY	143
FINAL WORDS	151

PROLOUGE
OCTOBER, 2016

"Who's there?" asked my dad as I knocked frantically on his door.

"Papa, it's me! Open the door quickly. I have a surprise for you.

He opened the door and asked, "What happened? Why are you guys shouting like animals?

My brother Sahil and I looked at each other, smiled, and exchanged a knowing look. Then we bent down and touched my dad's feet to receive his blessings. Sahil called our mom, who came out hurriedly from the kitchen where she spent half of her life.

We touched her feet too and took them to front yard of our house. I pointed to an XUV 500 car and said, "This is my gift to you." My dad had always dreamed of owning this car but could never afford one because of us (his family). My parents have made an infinite number of sacrifices and I believe yours have done likewise. My mom and dad were very happy at seeing our new and very first car. I saw surprise on their faces and a feeling on contentment at the same time. They praised us for our work. My mom gave me a pat on my shoulder and hugged me.

Then I turned to my dad and gave him the key to the car saying, "I'm sorry." I felt remorse for wasting a lot of his earnings on my business when I was just a beginner with silly and stupid ideas that never generated any profit but always made me disappointed, tired, frustrated, and tormented with a lot of reasons to quit. Thank God I didn't lose hope; otherwise, I would never have lived that wonderful moment. The moment I gave him the key and said, "It is my first tribute to you," tears rolled down his cheek and he hugged me tightly. The best thing I'd ever heard was what he said next: "I'm proud of you my son, I'm blessed to have sons like you both, I love you both, my heroes."

That was THE PROUDEST MOMENT for me because MY HERO was calling me his. Isn't it great?

Later that day, the four of us sat in our new car and excitedly went for a ride. My mom was sitting in a four-wheeler for the very first time, and she was on cloud 9.

When you make your dad and mom happy, you get the best feeling of accomplishment in the world. Your parents work so hard and make many sacrifices for you from the moment you're born. They give you all the happiness you desire, but when you get the chance to give them all that they longed for but went without for you, you need to selflessly provide for them when you get to earn. Money does play an important role in anyone's life. No doubt, there are things that money can't buy, but *IT CAN BUY MOST OF IT*. So, I wanted to make the fullest use of my earnings to bring happiness to my parents. And our good days began like this.

Fast forward to February 2017. My family and I are at the dining table, discussing this book.

My mother said, "We have two cars, one flat, and two bungalows. Also, you have enough financial stability, son, at such a young age of 18. I can't believe this. You're one in a million. You should always be thankful to everyone and everything around you.

"Hmm...! Yes, ma! You're right. I'm thankful to everyone," I agreed.

"Be thankful to me more than anyone else," said Sahil, giggling.

"Yeah Yeah, why not?" I joked. "You're the only person on this planet who should be thanked for everything in this world!" I winked and smiled back at him.

My father said, "Jokes apart. It'd better that you should always be thankful and try to motivate everyone. Your story is seriously one in a million. Why don't you write blogs or notes somewhere so that people can get inspiration from your story because, trust me, yours is very inspiring.

Sahil countered, "But no more than a hundred people would read that blog. I don't think it's a good idea if you really want to motivate and inspire people through your story."

Dad replied, "You're both on the Internet a lot. Think outside of the box and get an idea to narrate your story on a platform where more people can get to know that tough times are only a phase of life. People who are facing tough times, whose lives have become a nightmare, and who aren't seeing any ray of hope down the line might get inspired from reading about your journey.

"Yes, write a book!" my mom added.

"BOOK?" I questioned. "Oh yes, an eBook! Yes, I got it! I can write an eBook.

"Yes, that's a great idea," encouraged Sahil.

"I don't understand anything about Internet, so I can't suggest anything but can only say go for it," my dad said. My blessings are always with you. All the Best!"

"Thank you, Dad."

The following morning, I called Vikrant Shaurya an online publisher and introduced myself, saying, "Hello, I'm Shubham speaking. I'm an entrepreneur. I have a stable online business."

"Yes, Vikrant Shaurya here! How can I help you, sir?"

I said, "I want to write an eBook revealing everything I faced, both good and bad times. I feel my real story is quite motivational and it can help readers to feel positive about their life and keep them motivated even in tough times. I went through a lot of ups and downs in life. My life is a journey from grief to glory. I'm just 18 and have achieved a lot and successfully making millions of dollars with my business. I'd like to know whether or not my story has a marketable audience that will benefit from reading it and whether or not you can publish it.

Vikrant replied, "Sir, for that, you'll have to tell me your story because I have to at least have a synopsis of your story in order to know whether it's valuable or not? Only then can I assure you of anything. If you don't mind, can you find a time to tell your story to me?"

"Are you free today?" I asked.

"I have a meeting at 9:00 A.M. but I'm free after 11:00.

"I can meet you at Cafe Coffee Day at noon."

"I'll be there, sir. See you," said Vikrant.

At the coffee shop, Vikrant and I exchanged pleasantries and then got down to business.

"So, tell me how your story goes?" asked Vikrant.

"I replied, "My story goes like this................"

CHAPTER - 1
HOW IT ALL STARTED

I'm from the small town of Jharkhand, Dhanbad, a place where we greet one another with a smile.

The great thing about being raised in a small town is that my morals and values have been cultivated from day one, and at such a young age of 18, I can honestly say that these morals and values helped me to become the person I am today.

I belong to a lower middle class family where we never ate on a dining table. My family background wasn't good but better than a poor family. My father struggled all his life for his family. He was a shopkeeper who had a small shop that he managed to run along with his brother (my uncle) who together used to earn a salary of fifteen thousand per month, which was only enough to enable their family to survive and provide them with the basic needs of life. We were living in a government quarter, which was in the name of my grandfather, who was a retired government employee. He moved to his village, giving his two sons this quarter so that they could keep their family in town and provide his grandchildren with a proper education. We lived in a government quarter where ceilings were patched and two of the walls were a bit collapsed. We only wished to have our own house in a good condition of course.

My father was too social and he always wanted my brother, my two female cousins, and I to get a proper education. My parents always wanted us to become a respected and dignified people. That's why he and my uncle admitted the four of us to a good school in our city. He and my uncle used to invest most of their earnings on our education. Whatever we wanted and needed, my father took utmost care of everything, especially when it came to educational materials.

I always noticed the infinite sacrifices that my dad, my uncle, and my mom had made for us. They've enabled us to accomplish our dreams and well-being by virtue of their sacrifices. Thus, I was too inclined towards taking up a good job in my life so that I could start earning a handsome salary and give a helping hand to my father as soon as possible. I wanted to take the responsibility of my house, put them on my shoulders, and give my father a relief from each and every burden. My parents and uncle never enjoyed their life at all for our sake. They've been loaded with plethora of roles and responsibilities for my brother and me and our two cousins for a long time and not thinking about their own life. I really wanted to give them back their life and happiness by taking up some or all of their innumerable responsibilities.

I was the kind of boy who started thinking of these things from a very early age, and, since I was too young to get serious about life, I was unable to make up my mind to choose my career. I had no idea about what field actually attracted me, and what profession I should choose.

WHAT IS MY AIM?

I still remember the day when I went to my school to collect my report card of class 8th. I was promoted to class 9th. I turned my report card over to see my grades and remarks for my co-curricular activities. To my surprise, at the column of "AIM" was written "IITian," about which I knew nothing. When I inquired about this, a few of my friends told me that he asked everyone this question in the very last lecture of the class, and, since I was absent, my class teacher himself wrote "IITian" in the column of "AIM." I don't know what made him to do so, and while I was brainstorming about it, I summoned the courage to ask him the meaning of "IITian" and who is one?

So, I went to my teacher to ask about this and to satisfy my curiosity. He fortunately told me something that truly encouraged me a great deal. He first boosted my confidence by telling me that I was good at my studies, and then advised me to become an IITian. I heard this word for the very first time. I asked him about IITian. He told me, "IITian is a guy or a girl who puts in a lot of effort, dedication, and time to fulfil their dreams of getting into the 'premier' institute of engineering in India. IITian is basically an engineer, a most desirable one who's smarter, more passionate, and harder working than a common engineer. Very few students crack that IIT-JEE exam, and they become an engineer after four years of their academic study in IIT (Indian Institute of Technology). They're respected people and highly in demand in every technology. You just have to work hard and study day & night. Most importantly, they earn handsomely. If you become an IITian, you can fulfill your parent's dreams & desires." He encouraged me, using the nicest words and told me that I could do it for sure if I make up my mind. This was enough for me to start thinking about the engineering world. I smiled and thanked him for his suggestion as I prepared to take my leave.

Actually, an unfabled story is that my class teacher was a math teacher. His inclination towards technical studies wasn't hidden from anyone in the school. He always had a soft spot for engineering and technology and that's exactly where he guided all his students to go.

I thought about it for a long time after coming back from my school. I told my mom that I want to be an IITian. My mom too wasn't aware of this profession before. Actually NO, she knew what an engineer was but *IITian* was word she was unaware of. Since she always has known that there are only two great professions, doctor and engineer, she asked me, "What's that? I always wanted you to be an engineer or a doctor. Why do you want to become Ii... whatever you said?" I laughed and said, "Mummy, that's engineer only. My teacher told me about it and he believed I could do this. Imagine your son to be enrolled in IIT and becoming a top engineer. My innocent mother smiled after that. Maybe she started imagining me as an engineer from that very moment. I told her I would make her and dad proud one day.

ENGINEERING MANIA

WOW! I got 10 CGPA in class 10th. Yes, you read it right. I got 10 CGPA in matriculation (10th standard). Mom, Dad and Sahil (my brother) were happy. We partied, celebrated, and my father distributed sweets in our neighbourhood. My father and mother were calling all the relatives to inform them about my marks. Everyone was amazed. All of them gave me blessings and wished me luck for my future endeavours. Indeed all were advising me to work the same way or harder in my higher education and life too.

I was happy and I thought that studying, getting good marks, and making a career in a field like I was choosing was my cup of tea. I was confident enough and opted for engineering field as my career without giving a second thought about it and without being crystal clear about the things behind the mental scene (a bitter truth). All my friends were going to prepare for engineering, so, I too went on with that idea. I didn't know myself properly, so I stuck myself in a rat race because of my immaturity.

My father asked me about my next plan, what I was up to, what I wanted to do, and where I wanted to take admission for my further studies. I told him that I'd like to go to Patna (capital of Bihar) to prepare for the IIT exam. He kept silent for few minutes, thinking of how he would manage to send me, what my expenditures would be there in a different city living on my own, and whether or not he would be able to afford it? Obviously, a lot of expenses were required to send me to another place to study. My institute fees were 50,000 INR per year. I also needed a lot for my books, hostel, and school. Besides these investments, my family had living expenses too. My father and uncle faced a challenge to pay a lot of my expenses with only one shop as a mean of income for a family of seven members.

My uncle played a huge role in initially setting me on my career path. He made my father agree to letting me do what I wanted to.

Since, they had no money to pay for my fees of institute and hostel or for expensive books, they went to my grandfather for help. My grandfather was a retired government employee who had some savings in his account. Without thinking about anything else, he got ready to give all his savings for my education forthwith with the influx of hope that his grandson will become educated well enough to procure a prominent job.

I was too excited to go and take my first step in that particular direction where my teacher directed me once. All my friends were also heading for the same. Even those students who were not so good in studies opted for the same field and decided to move for preparation. I thought I could do it because if lower graders can desire for bigger dreams, why can't I crack that exam. I took SCIENCE stream for secondary education and moved to Patna from Dhanbad. I was unaware that Patna had something very different (from what I thought for myself) in store for me.

TRAIN TO PATNA

I, along with my uncle, reached Patna in the month of May 2014. My uncle, too, started dreaming for me. He, dad, and mom eagerly wanted to see me as an IITian. My uncle was doing everything to help me realise my dream.

Although my parents were very supportive and encouraging, I knew they were worried about the condition of our government quarter. Its ceiling was in a deplorable condition, as it was collapsed. Our ceilings were patched and few of ceiling patches had fallen down apparently. So, the ceiling dripped water inside the house every time it rained. Thus, during the rainy season, we had to keep a bucket to catch the water. My father and uncle wanted to do something about the leaky ceiling, but they were helpless. They couldn't afford to fix it as they had no savings. He and my uncle were the only earning men in our family with only one shop as a source of income and with a lot of responsibilities on their shoulders. All their monthly earnings were getting invested in our survival or in fees for their four children. My mother always wanted a house (our own house) with no repair problems. These things were always in my mind. I really wanted to solve this problem as soon as possible by any means.

I got admitted to a top coaching centre and started preparing for the IIT-JEE, an engineering exam that I wanted to crack. I was amused to see that thousands of students were there with the same idea and hope of cracking IIT-JEE and getting established with a good job. They were all a good scorer of matriculation and the teachers in Patna liked everyone's performance. The thousands of students were only in my particular coaching centre, but there were other coaching centres in the country for the same reason. So, millions of students were preparing for the IIT-JEE. I heard that the IIT-JEE exam was really tough, but I was a top student, so I thought it would be easy for me. I was totally unaware of the fact that engineering would not work out for me. Other students were doing well, but I was just in a rat race, not knowing where I was headed. Every increase in the number of students decreased my chances of becoming successful in this field. Still, I managed not to look back and moved forward trusting my dream & my ability to achieve it.

The next day, when my uncle was about to leave, he told me, "Work hard, nephew, and be an example for Sahil, so that he too will get good grades and becomes like you. I want you both to do what your father and I couldn't do because of financial crisis. Whatever you'll need, your father and I will provide it for you. Just call us for anything you require for your dream without any hesitation and, most importantly, focus on your studies.

I nodded, apparently contented with the promise, and calmly answered my uncle, "I Will."

Leaving my family and comfort zone scared the crap out of me. I found out that it would be really tough to live away from my family at a young age of 15, especially when I was doing it for the very first time in my life. I was homesick for weeks.

I started feeling uncomfortable about my father having to send me some of his earnings for my upkeep or other expenses. I never liked asking for money from home to meet my personal needs. So, I had an idea of getting a part time job to at least help my family a bit by not asking for money every week.

I always liked surfing the Internet for getting any information or reading about any relevant thing. I thought of searching for a mean of income on the Web. I asked a friend to borrow his laptop because I didn't have a laptop. I searched for any kind of work so that I could earn some money. I found many but I selected one means on Quikr that gave me a good idea about how the work was done there and how I could earn 5,000 per month, which was more than enough for my personal needs. So, I thought I'd go with that option. Through Quikr, I found out where I had to go to get registered. I went with my friend to the venue. There, I found out that I have to submit 2,500 in INR at the time of registration, which I didn't have. So, we returned to the hostel. In the evening, I called my father to ask for the money. He enquired the purpose that the large sum and I lied, giving him a lame excuse. It dejected him but he agreed. He deposited 2,500 in my account. I thought I would return this money to my father after I got my first salary because this money wasn't for education purpose. It was for something that my father was totally unaware of. I registered my name there to start my work in my leisure time.

A seminar was held about the online business, and I attended it. There were 15 to 20 people from whom I got to know about the business. I realized that the work that I was getting involved in was actually MLM (i.e., multi-level marketing. After registering my name there, the very first thing that I needed was a computer. With no idea of where to go for help, I simply called my dad. My mom picked up the call and she started asking about my livelihood here in the hostel. I told her about the pathetic condition of the hostel that I was living with. But mess was an upscale mess, mind you. There were no meals at times, no water once or twice a week, no proper aid to provide medical services when you're unwell, and mosquitoes. For the overpriced cost they charged, I had expected perfection to be honest. I just lived there so that I could prepare for my competition; otherwise, nothing could tempt me to stay there anytime. Eventually, from the time I started living there, I had been falling sick a lot.

After a moment of chitchat, I told my mother that I wanted to buy a laptop. It would cost nearly Rs. 28,000. When she heard that, she became sad. Though I knew the wretched condition of my home, my mom still explained their situation. She said, "Son nothing is hidden from you." You know your dad and uncle together make one small shop run, and their earnings are just Rs. 15,000 per month. We live in a joint family, with seven member living together. With such a small sum, we're unable to meet our basic necessities; still, we somehow managed to send you there to let you follow your dreams. How can you expect 28,000 for a laptop at this point of time?"

When I said nothing to her question, she asked me to get help from any of my friends so that I could commence my work. I replied with one word "okay," then said goodbye and I hung up the phone.

Thereafter, I asked my roommate if he could lend me his laptop for an hour every day. He enquired about few things first, but, since he knew my financial problem, he agreed. He asked a lot of questions about my work on Web and suggested that I shouldn't get into these things. He continuously gave his views about Internet work being a scam. He kept on telling me just to study instead getting trapped in any other thing. It took me couple of hours to tell him everything and to make him understand my need for a part-time job. Finally, he agreed to lend me his laptop every day but asked me to get my own Internet connection and to finance data usage.

Soon after commencing work, I wanted to quit, as I

had made no money, even after working for a month. But my mind guided me to carry on and have patience because it takes time to make money. I trusted my mind and believed that I would start earning money after a few more weeks in it. So, I kept doing it. Besides multilevel marketing, I kept on surfing the Internet most of the time whenever my friend left his laptop with me. From that, I gradually started learning about the online business. I learnt that some online marketers make millions and are leading luxurious lives. I got very interested in it and started learning more about that field.

My poor financial condition made me work to earn money. I invested in MLM by mistake, but it was too boggy. Because of MLM, I got distracted from my studies. I, an A-grade student, turned into an average student and then into a poor student. Now, I wasn't into studying at all, and that's how my marks started getting lower day by day. One thing for sure was that I got more interested in the Web world than studying and was becoming too friendly with the Internet day by day. I started giving more importance and attention to MLM than academic studies.

All the other students were great in their studies. They

were all diligent. I felt like my class was full of BRIGHT STUDENTS, except me, and I started losing my confidence. Everywhere around me, students were talking about alpha, beta, gamma, integration, differentiation, molar mass, kinetic energy, etc. (all were the terms of different subjects that we had to deal with (in our Science Stream). The more I heard these talks, the more I was getting frustrated and irritated with science, math, chemistry, and the whole B.Tech world. All my confidence went away and I suffered from an inferiority complex for a long time. All my hopes of getting selected for engineering and making a good career by studying harder were shattered. Being from a lower middle class family, the expectations and academic failure frustrated me, and I literally lost my mental balance to some extent. I couldn't give my best, but I kept on trying.

WAS IT AN ILLUSION?

Exam of class 11th was held, and I could only manage to score passing marks. I was among the lowest scorers of my class. It was a pathetic feeling. I really felt ashamed of my poor marks. I wasn't getting any idea to escape from this fact. This low mark of mine affected me a lot and I lost confidence of surviving in this countdown of becoming an engineer. The dream of my family to see me as an engineer became fanciful now. I felt like a reckless boy who made his family's investment in him an extravagance.

I was unable to tell my parents about all of this. I never wanted them to become aware of it because they trusted me to be studious and crack the biggest exam of engineering. Being the eldest son of my family, I had a lot of responsibility upon me. My parents always believed that I would help them lead a good life afterwards and that's why they invested in me. They gave me everything I needed. They sent me to Patna to study, but I broke their trust on my part. They might feel hopeless if they knew that what they had been sacrificing a lot for was going in vain now. Their son wasn't giving his best in that new city. Somehow, I made an excuse at home regarding exams and avoided telling them about what was happening.

My parent's hope, trust, sacrifices, and immense investment upon me was haunting me. Was I wasting my father's money, living away from home, doing nothing, and not even studying to get good marks? I sat in one corner and recalled everything that my family and I went through before coming to Patna. I consoled myself and gave myself one more chance to try again and to come back better because the final exam was still there to score and to keep my family's dream alive. I moved on and started studying harder.

But oh "Poor me"! The final exams held and I scored poorly again. Yes, I passed each time but just passing in this competitive world isn't enough.

I was wasting my father's income and wasting my time in stupid and silly things that I could never get back. There was no profit in work that I kept doing for few months. I wasn't able to score good marks in any semester exams. I must tell you, one can deal with one shock that come to you in one field but second, third and fourth consecutive shocks again and again in everything that you've been doing for longer makes it tough to recover. I wasn't like this earlier. I was a good student earlier. I used to score good grades. But what I face for the first few months was unexpected. The confidence that you lose at such a time is a huge loss. Unless you get a positive outcome, you can't gain that confidence back ever. You start doubting yourself and your abilities, and lose self-esteem. Failure even after hard and steady work in a field that I was once good at a few months back (got 10/10 in matriculation) was a biggest punch for me, as it shook my confidence that time. Confidence is like trust, easy to lose but tough to regain.

LIFE-CHANGING DECISION

Yes, I was left in torment. I got disheartened. All my friends got better marks than I did. No one teased me for my marks but everyone's behaviour changed towards me. None of my friends were now interested to call me for a group study or discussion, as they considered me a total waste of time. So, I started feeling intimidated. The feeling of inferiority was making me think of giving up. *My continuous poor marks falsified my opinion of myself as a good student.*

One night, I sat in my room in the hostel with the lights off, thinking of many things. I had many questions that I asked my inner self. Can I ever be able to crack IIT-JEE? Forget IIT; is getting a good rank in AIEEE (another engineering exam) my cup of tea? How will I ever pass my intermediate level exam like this? Am I really interested in this engineering thing? If I'm really interested, then why couldn't I get good marks in the two semesters, despite working harder?

The real picture behind these things was that I my teacher influenced me to take up this field. I wasn't interested in getting an engineering degree and getting a job in which I had to do monotonous things. I was living in an illusion that becoming IITian was what I actually wanted. Actually, I never wanted to live a boring life. I just thought of it because of my class teacher, who advised me once when I was too young to decide what I want to be, and because of my friends who were going after this field of engineering. I was stuck in a rat race and opted for a wrong field. I had two options left. The first option was to study, study, and study well. The second option was to follow my passion, entering into the Internet world and earn money.

I definitely wanted to earn enough to give all the happiness to my family and to take them out of that government quarter but, at the same time, *I wanted a kind of future that was rewarding, fulfilling, and satisfying. I wanted to be an entrepreneur.* There was a real Shubham inside me who never wanted to work for anyone. I wanted to work for myself. I always wanted to go for a job where I could be a boss. I wanted to explore my very own ideas. I wanted my own established company, and I wanted to have a life full of excitement and curiosity to crave for more. I was full of ideas from the start, so it was better that I should become someone who could implement ideas. I wanted my life to be more fun. On one hand, I wanted to fulfil my family's desire to see me become successful. On the other hand, I wanted to do something different. I didn't want to be an ordinary man. I wanted to stand out in any crowd. I wanted to start earning sooner to give my family financial support. I knew that 99% of people only dream of becoming successful in their respective area of interest and 1% are successful with what their desire. I wanted to be part of that 1% but if that were the case, then I wouldn't make it with what I was doing presently. As a result, I decided to not continue with the engineering preparation. I realized that even if I studied hard, I knew I couldn't become a good engineer because I lacked knowledge and motivation. But I knew that I could become a successful businessman if I gave it a try, as I had a lot of knowledge about this online business, and, more than that, I was passionate about becoming an online marketer and eager to learn more about the business world.

Knowing yourself better is an ecstatic feeling. Everyone should spend some time on their own to know and understand themselves better. The better you understand yourself, the better decision you make.

Now, my head became filled with thoughts, ideas, and refined facts & figures. I got a clear concept of everything. I realized that I was just wasting my father's money and my precious time by focusing on what I wasn't interested in at all. I always wanted to fulfil my promises to my dad, but I got to know that by doing this, I could never secure a good mark and could never get anywhere my dad wanted me to be. Preparing for and investing money on something I wasn't interested in was so unnecessarily extravagant. So, I decided something really BIG.

I was determined to go back to Dhanbad now and start a business. I was confident that my parent would support me because they were very understanding. Yes, I knew that it would definitely take time to make them understand what I really want and what my inner self asked me to do. But I was sure I could make them to understand sooner. I just needed to be confident on my part of becoming successful in my life and making miracles happen with what I was thinking to do. I knew this step was going be very crucial and important for me and could be a turning point of my life, but only if I made it happen.

I read it somewhere that *even the greatest leaders fail from time to time but the best ones think differently about failure than the rest of us.* Additionally, another quote that I read was *"Better be late than never!"* I took these lines to heart.

Without giving any second thoughts about it, I left my preparation and returned to my hometown the next morning. Yes, I'm a drop out because I wanted a kind of future that's rewarding, fulfilling, and satisfying. I wanted to fulfil my promises to my dad to make him proud, but this way, I could never be able to do so.

CHAPTER - 2
SAY 'NO' SO YOUR 'YESES' HAVE MORE OOMPH

January 2014.

I reached my hometown, Dhanbad. My mother was in the kitchen when I arrived home. She thought I was on a vacation. She was very happy seeing her son home and hugged me. I didn't say anything to her, as I wanted to tell both my parents at the same time. She made my favourite rice pudding as dessert that day. She bestowed lots of love on me and asked me a lot of question regarding my studies, friends, and Patna. I answered her every question calmly, but inside, I was just lost in collecting thoughts about what I would say to my father, mother, and uncle. I was building up courage to confront and face the situation. Whether they would get angry and what they would say were questions I was battling in my head. What would my brother think? These things were continuously revolving inside my head.

I was waiting for my father and uncle to come back from their shop. I must tell you, that day was far longer than other normal days. I was restless, since I had no idea how they would react after I told them about my plans. In the late evening, both of them returned home. They were surprised to see me at home. I touched their feet one after the other. They got freshened up. We sat together for dinner. They started a conversation and asked me about my sudden arrival. I was scared, so I started stammering. Still, I managed to speak. I told them about everything that I decided the day before, and the moment I told them about my decision to drop out of engineering, the silence was deafening. They remained quiet for few minutes and the silence broke when my uncle asked "If not engineering, then what?" I gave an immediate response that I want to start an online business.

My father got extremely angry after hearing my plan and decision. He declared that my decision was childish and baseless. He pointed at me and said to uncle, "Look at him. What's he saying? You persuaded me to send him to school, taking help from his old grandfather who's living in the village and has nothing for security there. He gave freely everything he had saved all his life to him. We trusted him and his dream, and this is what he's giving us back." I interrupted, saying that engineering wasn't my dream but what I decided lately was.

In anger, he immediately replied back, "And you were playing with our emotions and trust for so long? You're going to opt in for this frivolous career option over engineering. Do you have any idea what you're doing? You're just wasting time, money, and effort thinking of these silly things." I replied, "I know I've wasted a lot of money doing what I shouldn't have done. I'm sorry for that. But now, I don't want to waste money, time, and effort there in Patna doing something that doesn't interest me. Online business is what I really want to try. Please, understand me. I'm passionate about this, Dad, and here it's not wasting time, money, and effort, but it's investment. I was too young to decide what career field to adopt and in hurry. I made a wrong choice. It was just an illusion, but now I'm serious about this. I've had a lot of introspection and calculated all the pros and cons, and, trust me, I genuinely am interested in this now. Just give me one more chance. Trust me once more. This time, I won't give you any reason to complain."

We had nonstop arguments after that. Fierce arguments continued till the next day. He made me count all the mistakes I'd committed in the past. Tears rolled down my cheeks because, at that time, I wasn't seeing their trust on me. But that was okay because I felt it was fair actually. No doubt, I created a mess. I made a blunder. They were hurt. They had the right to scold me if they felt I was wrong. So, it was okay. My dad was still angry. It was very difficult for him to think of a good career with a low academic profile. My uncle went the extra mile again and took an initiative to propitiate my father for me. I was grateful to him for doing this and will always be obliged to him for the same. He told my father, "Subham is serious. He's your son, and I think you should give him this last chance and not be so harsh on him. If he quits this time, then I won't say anything. Thereafter, you're free to make him do whatever you want to." My father calmed down. Then my uncle asked me to explain further.

I made them understand the importance of the online business I wanted to venture into. I explained to them that the world was becoming more and more technologically advanced. The Internet had created a new economy that, by its explosive growth and sheer size, had surprised everyone in the world. It had changed the perception of traditional way of doing business. Getting online was becoming cheaper and easier because of emergence of new technologies. I told them that I could instantly be a global player with e-business. I didn't ignore the fact that marketing on the Web was expensive because of competition, but I could successfully do it due to my potentials.

I tried everything to convince them because their support and blessings were really important to me. I wanted them to have trust in me. I told them all the benefits of getting into online marketing that were known to me. I told them about how and why the Internet was the best platform for the betterment of any business, how Internet made information more easily available to customers, how it provided better customer support. I also included that with online business, I will have the ability to do business 24/7. Moreover, it had low start-up costs, I could go global, and my physical presence could be in any location.

On the first note, I was fearful and was expecting a negative response from them and intense interrogation with too many questions I didn't have answers to, but, to my surprise, none of my family member asked questions. They didn't even discourage me or give any comment that would make me feel that I wasn't being productive to the family and for my own sake. Instead, the responses I received posed that my decision was welcoming. My family didn't come with trigger warnings. Yes, they only wanted to know about my work. The little anxiety and curiosity that they showed in order to know what their boy was going to do in the future was innocuous. It was fine. It was good, actually, because you feel that your family understands you and your work and supports you in it. Family's support for me was the foundation to my career path.

I also assured them that I would definitely complete my higher secondary education but from an open school. Besides, I made it crystal clear that I would make my career in the online business world only and my education was just a formality for their happiness. This decision was all mine and I seemed to be highly passionate about adopting this as my career. So, they didn't force me to do anything. They accepted the fact completely and took me and my interest seriously. I have to mention that I was lucky to get a supportive family. My mom and uncle wished me the best of luck and asked me to work hard and do well, and my father said only one sentence: "We trust you my child. Don't quit this time, and do make us feel proud."

Now I had no choice left other than becoming successful in this field. The options I had were either TO DO IT or TO DO IT.

CHALLENGE ACCEPTED

I was done with the first step, as I got approval from my family. Now, I was all good to move to the next stage. But before that stage, I was faced with another hurdle. I only had a second-hand desktop computer at my place, which was in terrible condition. Its motherboard was too old. A display was connected to the computer, but it couldn't display anything. Even if it worked sometime, it was slow. The computer speaker also wasn't working properly. Even some of the keys on the keyboard weren't working. I went to the computer service centre to repair it. My computer wasn't totally prepared, but it was now rough and ready to go. If I used it to work for more than an hour at a time, it would get too hot and stop working. As was truly said, *"When in deep crisis, one resorts to all means, fair and unfair."*

After its repair (semirepair actually), I got 2G Internet connection because 3G was too expensive for me. I started researching every tidbit of online business. The key, regardless of what type of business you're starting, is to be flexible. If you want everything else to go as smoothly as possible, you'll need to prepare. Every business needs consumers for its products and services. Doing a business isn't as easy as its spelling is. The right determinant of e-business success is the same as any offline business. You need to begin with a great idea, and then develop a business plan. There should be a value proposition for prospective clients, and you should have a belief in it and in your ability.

There's too much to know before you take any initiative in this field. There are many important phases if you peep inside the business world, especially when it's online. One needs to research a lot and plan first, and then you have to target your market and determine who your potential clients will be, what specific products or services you'll offer to draw them in. At this point, I was totally a newbie who definitely had enthusiasm and dream in his eyes but lacked ideas and ways for moving ahead.

In the month of February, I checked some online income streams. I found out that I needed to have at least a PayPal account and a credit card. Since I wasn't 18, I used my mother's name to registering for a PayPal account to continue. I was about to open an account there on my computer but oh, poor me! Only one month after my computer's repair, it again started creating a mess for me in my working strategy by shutting down automatically whenever I worked with it for a long time. So again, I gave my computer to a technician for repairing. I had to open my mother's PayPal account in a cyber cafe because of my impaired computer.

After creating the PayPal account, I was asked to add my credit card information to my account. PayPal definitely stores and safeguards card details, but I didn't have any credit card. I had two debit cards, but both of them weren't allowed to be linked to my

PayPal account. PayPal enables online trading and supports either a credit card or international debit cards of any private banks for instance ICICI, HDFC, or AXIS bank.

I wasn't eligible to get a credit card because I wasn't 18 (underage). Also, I didn't have any source of income to show to the bank. So, after discussing this problem with my uncle, we came to a conclusion that he would get a credit card and I would use it for my business purposes. My uncle had his account in SBI bank. He applied for a credit card. In a couple of weeks, he got his credit card for me. I linked it to my PayPal account and started using his card to work then.

I learnt the hard way that MLM was a trap, so I decided never to get into that again. I began with a lot of research and trial. I started surfing the Internet about many ideas. After spending a lot of time studying Internet marketing, affiliate marketing, and online marketing, I was good to go into this world. I took my first step with pay to click websites. Pay to click was easy to start and I read that even a neophyte could start generating income from the very first day as it required less skill to work. I thought of staying in a comfort zone while starting fresh. I invested around 2,000 in Indian rupees on a pay to click website. It gave me positive result for the first few days but, afterwards, it became useless. I realized that I was just wasting my time and money. Eventually, I left that platform with disappointment.

Then I came to know about online courses. One thing was common with all the courses. Every course claimed that you make money with lists. I started purchasing list-building courses. With those courses, I learnt a lot about right practices of running an online business. I understood the mechanisms behind building a list of email addresses. Those courses were helpful as I build my very own email list from scratch and created a subscriber database to leverage the reach of my business. I was then once more ready to get started.

Before I continue with my story, I should tell you what list building is. List building is the process of adding new subscribers to your mailing list. A subscriber gives you their email address in exchange for receiving certain information, a special offer, or a free gift. Once you have your email list, then you can sell them your products, service, or promote other products for commissions. An email list means a list of names of customers with their email addresses. Those emails that I was likely to send to my subscribers had been an opportunity for me to relate to my leads and to prove that I'm relevant.

I also learnt domain flipping (how to buy and sell domains), hosting, and building websites. I started building my own sales funnel. A sales funnel is a marketing system. It's the foundation of growth and revenue. The sales funnel visually describes the sales process from initial contact to final sale. It's the ideal process that one intends his/her customers to experience as they go from prospect to lead to customer to repeat buyer.

When I started research and learning sales funnel things, I used to stay at one of my friends place the whole day in order to use his computer for browsing and researching, as my system was at repair shop. It took one whole month in researching and then I was all prepared to take the initiative. My friend was appalled to see that I wasn't studying at all and kept on doing things day and night that has no security and stability. He always asked me to drop this idea of doing online business and concentrate on my studies to get a secure job after completing my studies because he always had seen me as a brilliant student in school days. He always encouraged me to complete my academic education properly rather than getting stuck in something that had no respect in the real world. I also told him about online business world. Still he kept on asking me to come out from an imaginary and virtual world. I never said anything after that. I just heard his views, smiled, and carried on with my researches.

Let me explain a sales funnel with an example. Did you know that it costs McDonalds $1.91 in advertising to get you into the drive through?

And when they sell you a burger for $2.09, they ONLY make $0.18.

But, when they upsell you fries and a coke for $1.77 more they make (and more importantly keep) $1.32 as profit.

Yes, eight times the profit of the initial sale!

Pretty cool, isn't it?

Suppose you're an online marketer and you sell your products online or promote products for commission.

You set up a website or a squeeze page and start driving traffic to it. But just like McDonalds, even if people are buying it, after your advertising costs, you're probably not left with enough to even cover your hosting bills.

And that's when you realize that if you want to make it online, you can't sell from a flat website.

You need to do what McDonalds did and setup a sales funnel.

But instead of having people go through a drive-through window, they go through a "capture page" where you can gather their contact information and follow up with them through email.

Then, instead of selling them a burger, you have a sales page created to sell your initial product.

And while you're probably not going to offer your customers any fries and a coke, you could upsell them on your other products and services.

This's what we call a "Sales-Funnel."

Where website visitors can come in the top and cash comes out of the bottom.

I was a quick learner, and that played a great role on me adapting to changes and being eager to learn new methods and procedures effectively. I started digging out more different ways in order to intensify the chances of increasing the number of subscribers. I started paid advertisements, free advertisements similar to what had been mentioned on those courses. I got positive outcomes as a result. I built around 2,000 to 3,000 subscribers but no income had been generated even though I invested 20,000 Rupees while making email lists. A big amount of an investment turned useless for me and it all went in vain producing not one single penny as an earning.

After that, I had to email my subscribers with potential and valuable content and build a relationship with them. Most importantly, I was supposed to build credibility with my subscribers for lasting effect of a relationship. I emailed and followed each and every advice that had been given in the course, step by step. I saw good responses and was happy with my work that I did then.

After that, similar to email marketing, I emailed my subscribers with some offer, hoping to earn some money online. I promoted several offers that had been launched by my online friends or affiliates but I failed miserably. I made zero bucks.

With the perception and expectation of generating some revenue, I started investing money. I saw the possibility of investing small amounts of money. So, I invested some money or online income streams through my PayPal and credit card. There's a difference between small and large investments (i.e., how big amounts of money changes revenue). I read somewhere that small amounts of investment in business works slow and possess less power to generate revenue. Your progress will be slow if you're investing small amounts. Investing small amount mean you have to wait longer to earn your dividends. With small amounts, you win only if you invest for a long period and if you look much further. People need to wait for a longer time but who wants to wait? I was investing money and hurriedly wanted my investment to bear fruit. I wanted to take their money back as quickly as possible because of insecurity and fear. I believed in what I was doing. So, I almost doubled my investment. Funds spent in that period brought no profit and went in vain. Despite good number of investments, the terrible news was that losses had been on the way. I faced losses after losses.

Undoubtedly, I was learning a lot during my trial period, but my mistakes were leading to heavy losses for me. By my mistake, I learnt that even though your progress will be slow with small investments, still you can reinvest your profits and grow your business, but arbitrary larger investment can tear you apart.

The financial condition of my family got worse than ever. They didn't make money yet they spent a lot of money on my studies and that alone was a money drain to anyone. Later, they gave me all the financial help I needed from them. They shelled out around one hundred thousand rupees when I was in Patna and again when I was in this e-Business thing, I wasted too much of my parent's money. I started feeling really bad for them. They too were worried about me and my work. I didn't know whether they doubted my abilities or not, but self-doubt questions started seeping inside me for sure. Wasting money after money and getting no result is a worst thing to face. I made no good money online till then, so I wasn't at a stage where I could give them financial assistance.

My brother, Sahil was a student of class 8th. He came to me and asked me to quit what I was doing (i.e., online entrepreneurship). He said if I will study and get a stable job then my career will be secured, whereas, I will become liable enough in giving my family a financial aid. He was saying I should get a job somewhere and leave this dream behind. He told me that I was made for a job and not for business. He advised me that doing business is lot more difficult and challenging. I replied to him calmly that no one is born for a job or business. Till the time we don't try on our own, how can anyone say what fits us better? I know I can do better in this field running my own business. Online business can drive me somewhere where people admire me for reaching; it will provide me with different opportunities online. Now, I was already in it and I would continue further until I achieved what I really wanted. I told him how Internet marketers are getting name and fame by doing what they really love to do and they do it in their own way. No one rules over them. He told me that, although online business can be rewarding for some, it could be very tedious and demanding for few.

I heard his views and perception about Internet marketing. Then I directed him to look at the bright side. I answered that it indeed takes an enormous amount of hard work, but that's just comes with the territory. It gives us something that's worth all of that. I explained to him about my work, giving him lots of valid reasons and showed him examples on Facebook to prove all my reasons. I made him read success stories of many online entrepreneurs who were earning six figures just in one month with this and they were all flourishing. Their stories and way of life enticed Sahil. He was amazed to see successful people's flourishing with online entrepreneurship. I saw in my brother's eyes a desire to be successful too; his eyes were glittering in amazement. Of course, the standard of living, way of working, and success of the examples I showed him were enviable for anyone. It definitely allured him in a way that must have influenced him to change his mind about Internet marketing.

After hearing me out with an open mind, he went away, giving me a gesture of "carry on."

One day, while I was sitting and surfing the Web, he come again and said something that surprised me. He wanted to work with me and carry on with online business. I had no problem with this. Besides, I would be getting a helping hand from someone I could trust. Whatever interested him and made him inclined towards this world, I was happy with his decision. He continued his studies and started devoting his spare time to online business with me. Both of us were in it now and started browsing the Web to learn about new Internet works, grasping more and more techniques, and getting specialization to get started.

DEAL WITH NEGATIVITY POSITIVELY

A few relatives and neighbours started to make disparaging remarks and taunt me about my work. They judged my work and abilities just by knowing that I left my studies and returned home to start a business that had no future. It did affect me a lot, but I pretended to be fine. My family also asked me to settle down fast because I had been at it for a long time.

I'd been feeling really bad for the past several months as I continued to fail towards reaching my desired goals. I was again in a state of confusion regarding my career. Self-doubt questions started seeping inside me. I started doubting my potentials. I felt like an absolute loser, an incurable zero. The constant stream of negative and pessimistic thoughts in my mind made me feel depressed, and that prevented me from doing any productive work or creative problem solving. After that, I started feeling depressed most of the time, thinking about my failures, not-so-good career, and having no money. I had pent-up anger such that even the slightest thing could set me off. When negative thoughts hit our brain, it's tempting to struggle with them in a never-ending thought loop. We need to break this loop with positive thinking.

When you're reluctant to step back and just want to move forward, heading in the right direction with confidence, you fight with negative thoughts, and then you learn the art of positive thinking. I breathed deeper to try and dispel the negative thoughts. I only intended to doze, to hover in peace, and to eliminate negative thoughts. I somehow managed to turn off the negative thoughts channel in my mind and develop my true potential with positive thoughts.

I completely gave a pause to my study in 2014. I didn't

even glance at my books that year. I hadn't even given a single thought about it till my final examination. I just got involved in my work.

I learnt two basic rules of life:

Rule 1 says Never Quit until you reach where you want to be.

Rule 2 says Always remember Rule 1.

That's it and I moved on and threw all negative remarks about me out of my life. From then on, I noticed that each detractor was doing nothing productive about their life and was just pulling me down by giving me an upsetting thought.

I already had a Facebook account but I created another Facebook account where no one knew me. I befriended people who were Internet marketers or were having an online business in something or other. My online friends there were all from different countries. I started chatting and networking with them, building healthy relationship with them. Facebook can be a great booster for a new entrepreneur if you're in a right direction. Facebook helps your large, medium, or small business grow. I learnt from them how things work out there.

Everyone out there had something to brag about. People frequently used to post updates telling their friends how blessed their career has been or screenshots-by-screenshots progress that they were leading to. Many of them wrote testimonials boasting about their luxurious life. Their life appeared so perfect that it sometimes annoyed me because I compared their lives with mine. Meanwhile, I was envious of their blissful and blessed life. Flashes of envy towards my Facebook friends doesn't mean that I was a bad or selfish person. Research shows that one gets an emotional boost when he or she feels like they're winning in life. Dealing with life's unfairness made me realize that I was feeling unimportant. So, after that realization, I took every friend's update sportingly and such posts encouraged me and motivated me to keep on working. I was friends not only with foreign entrepreneurs but I also built good relationships with Indian marketers as well. I was really good at building sales funnels; so, I helped other Indian marketers to improve their sales funnel and earn around 1,000 to 5,000 in INR.

Once conquering my negative thoughts, I changed my perception towards others' successful lives. Now, I absolutely always loved knowing about people who had succeeded despite failure and rejection. I got motivation from them. It feels good when you get to know that hard work does pay. It doesn't matter what extreme kind of hard times you faced one day; if you've worked really hard, you'll definitely achieve success either now or later but success is sure to come. At the same time, I used to feel anxious and restless wondering when exactly my time would come. People around me were all doing great in their lives with list building, affiliate marketing, and other online streams like CPA and tee-spring.

I was into list building before then I shifted my attention from list building to CPA (Cost per Action).

CPA is very simple; you get paid when someone clicks on your affiliate link and completes an action. The action can be just about anything but usually consists of filling out a form, getting an estimate or quote, signing up for a free trial, or buying something.

CPA generally involves risk for an advertiser, yet I wanted to try it out. While trying CPA, I again lost a huge amount of money. I was influenced by tee-spring marketing and I wanted to try it too. Tee-spring is a platform that makes it really easy for anyone to design high-quality T-shirts and sell them online by leveraging crowd funding and social media to make money.

You just have to design your T-shirt on tee-spring platform and then promote that campaign on social media. If you'll sell those T-shirts, tee-spring itself will print that T-shirt and ship it to the buyer's shipping address.

So, basically, you have your T-Shirt business running without having to pay for a T-shirt printing machine and shipping system. But by that time, I wasn't make any good amount of money from online business. Instead, I was losing money while trying one thing or another.

I was earning 3,000 to 4,000 Rupees through online work, but I had no money in my pocket by the end of the month. This was because I was purchasing a few online courses, so even my small earnings were literally getting used to keep my credit card's balance low and to manage my debt.

In 2014, I'd been too calculative and analytical the whole year. I used to plan a lot, speculating that if I got 2,000 subscribers, then I would be able to generate massive income and process another business strategy that would give me an effective result. My plans never became successful. Later, I no longer speculated, and the results I got were beyond my expectation. Even now, I run my business without speculation and I'm doing excellent

With a few bumps and bruises in my first year of hit

and miss, I learnt a lot. Even though I couldn't get any success with my plans yet, I didn't think any time was wasted, for in each failure is an opportunity to learn something and grow. The whole time, I learnt to track things that were valuable lessons for any business. The lessons learnt when you start a new business are just as important as the business you're building.

MY FIRST LOVE IS MY FIRST SALE OF $220

In the year 2015, Sahil and I started Fiverr in the month of January. When we started, we had zero feedbacks and referrals after our names. You must be wondering what zero referral mean. Let me tell you how Wikipedia defines Fiverr. "Fiverr is a global online marketplace offering tasks and services, beginning at a cost of $5 per job performed, from which it gets its name. The site is primarily used by freelancers who use Fiverr to offer services to customers worldwide." In a layman language, it's a global marketplace for buying and selling of services for as little as $5.

I created a gig on my Fiverr account where I had to create sales funnels for my clients. We were emotionally and financially broken because whatever strategy we made initially, it always went completely against our expectations and plans. No one wants to be broke. Being broke sucks. I've had extended periods in my life where I've been living on the edge of financial ruin, so I know how stressful and overwhelming it can be. When you're broke, things are much worse and damn depressing. It's hard to leave ANY option, regardless of how insanely miserable it is. But one thing is for sure. That is, being broke gave me an entirely different perspective on cash flow, debt, and my own financial well-being. We were hopeless about this as well. Still, we were doing this because there was no going back for us. I put in more effort and worked full-time.

While we were in the Fiverr world, I met a guy, Vik Pandey, on Facebook. He was an Internet marketer and was in partnership with an established Indian Internet marketer Jai Sharma. They had two successful Internet marketing products launched earlier. At that time, there were a lot of online tutorials and tutors from all the different fields of online marketing. But I wanted to get a tutor whom I could trust. I knew Vik and Jai, so, I approached them.

Vik Pandey told me that he and Jai Sharma could become my coach and were willing to guide me. They charged $1,000 for the coaching. I was financially broke and totally in torment. I wasn't getting any idea on what to do next and how to pay my fees to my coach, but I wanted to learn from them as they assured me that I could also launch, and that launch could bring me massive and passive incomes. It already had been so long for me but, still, there were no significant result coming forth. I really needed a push. I really wanted to get started with online massive income.

I had no choice other than going to my father and uncle to ask for help. I told my parents and uncle that I want to get Internet marketing coaching to learn things in detail. I told them how my coaches were earning daily and if I got the chance to learn from them, I too could earn handsomely. No one trusted me then. It didn't sound realistic to them. They refused to give me that big amount. I kept on asking for the money. I begged in front of them for help. I tried a lot to convince them, but they didn't agree. After a couple of days, I didn't know what made them do so but my parents went to Muthoot Finance and took a loan of one hundred thousand rupees by mortgaging some gold jewellery of my mom. It was a really emotional time for me when I got to know this. What they did for their son was extremely priceless. I will never forget that ever in my life.

My parents' immense love for me can't be described in words. I was numb at that time, and even today, I'm unable to express how I really feel about that. I just can't express how blessed I am to have parents like them. They didn't always let me do what I felt was right, without ever bogging me down with restriction, but they also supported me with everything they could offer. They always gave me more than what I ever could have asked for. Their support has always been vital. I owe them a lot. I thanked them from the bottom of my heart. I promised my parents that I would get my mother's jewellery back as soon as possible.

As a result of that, I had to work harder, day and night. I needed positive thoughts. I just closed my ears and eyes because I never wanted to hear what others were saying about me and how they felt about my work. I kept myself motivated. There were Indian Internet marketers like Gaurab Borah and Jai Sharma whose stories always inspired me. Their successes were intrinsically unavoidable. I always told their stories and accomplishments to my parents. They were doing superbly in their lives. Whatever I got to know about them, be it buying a car, buying a villa, etc. gave me a motivation to stay in online business and to work harder each day. I gave my parents assurances that I would do the same for them. I just kept my head held high.

I knew almost everything about affiliate marketing. I didn't need any coaching that time. My brother and I knew it all, whatever was in that course. We both were good at technical skills. We just were looking for an established launcher who could launch with us. We just joined that coaching with only one hope that we would get an opportunity to launch some Internet marketing information products with Jai Sharma. I thought that even if I launched a single product with him and over one thousand customer placed orders for that product, then I could repay the money. That was my only intention for joining the coaching.

No, I'm not boasting about our talents. We were seriously amazing from the time we began. Even though we were trying to earn a living from online marketing, still we weren't succeeding in making money. We had nothing to do but just research and read about different thing that actually worked, and this was vital in online business. We used to spend hours surfing about everything in this field. As a result, we got to learn even the things that other entrepreneurs found complicated. We got all the required technical knowledge. We grasped everything superbly. We became web development virtuosos and pros in technical knowledge and were well aware of different things, including website building, Wordpress, plugins, and all website related matters.

I paid our fees of $1,000 to Jai Sharma and Vik Pandey. They scheduled the calls and I started talking to them for tutorials. The benefits of scheduling calls included facilitating communication and updates among us, discussing issues that we were facing, and brainstorming possible solutions. During the brainstorming sessions, we never discarded any ideas until they had been thoroughly discussed. We discussed every possible idea and executing plan.

March 2015 arrived. It was the month of my intermediate level (class 12th) final exam.

Up till that time, I still wasn't making any money. I really wanted to start making money as soon as possible, as that scenario was very threatening. I was scared because my final exam was less than a month away. I was 100% sure that I was going to fail because I didn't study, even for once from the time I entered the online business world. I knew my family would get hurt when they found out about my marks on the 12th exam, and they would definitely scold me for that. But more than that, I would lose credibility. They would never be able to trust me again and would doubt my competence. At that point of time, I didn't want them to lose their trust in me. I thought that if I start making money before the exam, then there was a chance that they might not be too angry at me. They might still trust me because they would see me doing fine at least with something in my life.

The day before my first day of examination, I went to my friend's place for group study. Yes, I went to study. I went to him to ask for important topics to study for the very next day examination. Actually, I wanted to know the quickest study strategy so that I could get the easiest way to deal with the monster called "exam." I asked him to summarize important points and let me understand each point's synopsis, so that I could get passing marks at least. He started giving me a summary of every chapter. At midnight, my brother, Sahil, called me when I was studying and informed me that we just got a sale of $20 on Fiverr. Our first sale on Fiverr was an order for building a sales funnel. I was very happy knowing this.

Again, within the next hour, I got another call. Sahil called me back. This time we got another sale of $200. We made 220 dollars that day. A ray of hope brightened my heart. These two sales gave a boost to my confidence. I was too happy and excitedly. I informed my friends and parents about the news. I was so happy and enthusiastic that I kept on exploring more ideas for more sales and my work, and, as a result, I was unable to focus on my studies. All my anxiety about my final exam just vanished and I didn't even touch my books. I didn't even try to study after that. I kept imagining and dreaming about more sales and a future luxurious life. I slept dreaming about a comfortable life, living on my own terms and conditions. The next morning, I woke up and ran towards my home hurriedly as I had to talk to Sahil. We discussed ways we would complete our customer's work. We were filled with energy. We wanted to fulfill our customer's desires to the best of our abilities so that we would have a long-lasting relationship with them as well as get positive feedback about our services that other potential customers could read on Fiverr.

Even though we had two orders for completion on a deadline, still I was relaxed and calm because I felt like I'd stepped up my game. I got work that bought us money. I felt more energetic and confident than ever before. I then went to take my exam without any stress and fear of failure.

CHAPTER - 3
BEGINNING OF A NEW ERA

March 2015

In a nutshell, I read the exam's questions and freaked out. I was totally blank and had no clue about what to write for answers. There's nothing quite like the sinking feeling that comes when you turn over an exam paper and realise that you know nothing to write about. I couldn't write more than one page on any question. All my exams went terribly bad..

I wasn't thinking about exams. Whilst it's understandable that if I had no reason to pass those exams and was fully inclined towards the work that I was doing to earn a living, then, of course, I took my exams lightly. I was totally against wasting my time and energy in what I had no passion for. I thought that there wasn't any point in having bookish knowledge occupy my precious mental space. Instead, there was something that was more worthwhile to me: Fiverr. Fiverr has been a lucrative platform for many online marketers, earning six plus figures a year. So, with that goal and dream in my eyes, I was more interested in and focused on it, and, more importantly, we were making good money with Fiverr.

The most important thing a service provider can do for their clients is to help them in generating long-term value. Keeping that in mind, our clients' interest always came first for us from the very beginning of our work. We had to give our clients quality work delivered to them under deadline, but our computer was in poor condition. It was slow and used to hang often. It was getting tougher for us to work on that desktop. So, we thought of buying a computer system with the money we were earning. We were running out of money, so we didn't want to drop a bunch of cash on one. We sat together and planned to get a great deal by buying second-hand laptop

My work was letting me earn good amount of cash, which I was investing on improving my family's living. We hired labourers and spent our earnings on repairing the ceiling. Finally, we got a better roof with ceiling that could help us not getting wet on the rainy days. My mom was really happy with this investment of ours. Slowly and slowly, by taking baby steps, I started fulfilling some needs and a few desires of my family. I sent money to my grandparents too. I started helping my family to improve their standard of living and was giving my best to rectify all the mistakes I had made. I started giving my family a sign of relief from financial crisis. My family was very happy with our work. They appreciated our efforts and talents, and those who had assumed that I would do nothing meaningful with my life were surprised by our accomplishments.

During my exam days, I bought a second-hand laptop. It was our first investment that we made on our own generated income. Things changed significantly. The way things used to work in the past wasn't the same for us anymore as our new laptop was faster and simpler to work with. Now, with the new laptop, we were able to implement our projects efficiently. We were fast and furious in dealing with the completion of our customers' work.

I lost interest and zeal in studying and had no time to prepare for any exam. My exams didn't bother me at all. I was carefree and working happily. My brother and I were fulfilling our clients' demands in the shortest time.

List building was something I already did earlier and was a total PRO at, as I had a lot of experience with it. Also, I helped many marketers too with this. I was a know-everything guy in that field. Because of the knowledge that I attained, I started getting students for list building. Sahil helped me a lot with this. He was the one who helped me creating gigs on Fiverr.

I got my first student on Facebook, who wanted me to teach him how to build lists and create good sales funnels. I was neither a famous list builder nor was I having my name anywhere on online marketing. But just because I managed to tell him a few things I knew about list building, he wanted to learn all the tricks and strategies from me. He agreed to get coaching from me and paid $397 for that. He joined me in the month of March. After that, two more students approached me. In total, three students were ready to take coaching from me.

In April 2015, I got two more students. I raised my fees of coaching by $100 and asked them to pay $497 each if they want to take coaching. Almost immediately, they agreed to that. I was doing very well with my online work and started earning a stable income by then. Beside this, I wanted to have a launch with Jai Sharma, so, I was into forming a healthier relationship with my coaches because I was trying to hand over my launch in few days. I wanted their suggestions for the launch and their help in building subscriber lists to promote affiliate products in order to make money from them as well. I succeeded with that too. I started calling my coaches, often to discuss the launches. They discussed with me and let me present my ideas and views because they were knew well known that I had a lot of technical knowledge about different online tools and genres. They also knew that Sahil and I never needed coaching in that at all.

ON-THE-JOB TRAINING

Next month, my mentor Jai Sharma asked me to visit his city, Delhi. He wanted me to work one on one with him. It was overwhelming to visit one who once was my inspiration. He was an Internet marketing star and was doing really good in his life. He developed a system to make his own money and his own Internet revenue. His professionalism and way of work always impressed me. I went to his place to learn from him. It was the first time I was meeting my 'teacher of work' in person. Previously, I always saw him virtually in pictures and talked with him in telephone conversations. It was very pleasant meeting with him and refreshing to work with him. I stayed there for almost a week. During my stay, I got to learn a lot from him.

He took me out for a meeting with one more Internet marketer who lived in Delhi. We reached Ambience Mall and met Vicky Sharma. While in the meeting, I found out that he, like me, was also from Bihar. I got a warm welcome from him. We talked about our living, family, online journey, our places, etc. There are few people in my life with whom I get close to in just my very first meeting with them. He was one of them. We also planned on collaborating for our business and growing it into a conglomerate. We were in touch from then on.

After my week in Delhi, I returned to my hometown. In the middle of May 2015, my intermediate result was about to be announced. I wasn't at all concerned about my result because I knew that my paper had gone terribly bad and under no circumstances would anyone pass me. *I thought what's gone is gone forever.* I never wanted to see my result. So, I didn't care about checking my result or the marks. Instead, I just carried on with my online day job. On the day of declaration of result, I was outside my home when my phone rang and Sahil's name flashed on its screen. This time, he called to give me the bad and disgusting news that I had failed in my intermediate examination. I expected it actually, but the only thing I was worried about was how my parents would react after finding out. My dad and uncle were strict about my studies and results. Still, they just offered me condolence while talking to me, telling me not to worry about anything relating to result because it didn't affect what I was doing presently. I was making great margins and paying ourselves well, so they too accepted the fact that school marks don't matter if you're doing your job successfully. In fact, they encouraged me, saying that what really matters is one's willingness to work hard even when failure comes and to achieve what one really dreamt of. Now, since my result didn't disturb any of my parents, failing to complete schooling didn't bother me either.

Our Fiverr work was generating good revenue and was giving a good result. In June 2015, I attained stability with online income. My brother and I were doing good and achieving our predicted income every month following our strategies. We were making about one hundred thousand rupees a month through our Fiverr business then. We never thought that we might aspire to greater heights. We were happy with what we got after facing a lot of struggle, difficult times, and gloomy days. I persistently tried to do my best in every situation and launching products added to my income. Apart from my Fiverr business, I was still working and trying to grasp more about affiliate marketing.

I had an online friend who lived in Bangalore. We chatted a lot and became very good friends. I'll call him "Bangalore guy" because I don't want to make his name public. One day, he expressed a desire to meet Sahil and me. He was an older man, about 40, more than double my age. He was making no money online but desperately wanted to. He insisted that we teach him ways to earn online. I thought of him as a great guy and friend. His curiosity, persistence, and desire to really learn about online business made me get ready to guide him and let him learn. I had no problem about teaching him what I already knew because I too once faced difficult times when there was no one to guide me and show me the right path that could lead me where I really wanted to. I had a soft spot in my heart for him because I could relate to what he was going through. I wanted his and his family's betterment. I wanted his financial condition to get better. I thought there wasn't any harm in giving a helping hand to a needy one. I thought maybe for this good deed without asking anything in return, I would be blessed and he would be my friend for life. Eventually, he paid us a visit.

After coming to our place and meeting us, he showed his inclination towards product launching. He said he wanted to launch a few products with me, and his only intention was to earn some money. He told us that he wanted our name to be there in the launch because we had good bonding with some successful marketers across the country; otherwise, his launch would fail. I agreed on that as well. I was doing everything for him because of our friendship.

He wanted to live with us, but we had a small government quarter. Not knowing where he could stay, we decided to get a rented room for him. He stayed there and we took proper care of him. But he took advantage of our kindness. His real motives were hidden from us, and he was playing dirty with us. His mind was preoccupied with some trivial objectives that could have bothered us later. This Bangalore guy was here to use us and exploit us. Unaware of the fact that he had negativity dwelling in his mind, I kept on helping him with whatever he required.

The three of us (Sahil, the Bangalore guy, and I) used to work together in that rented room. After spending a whole day with him, we realized that he was good for nothing. He was too lazy to work. He used to lie down on the bed the whole day long, doing stupid things or talking to us about petty issues and trifling matter. He was wasting our time by staying with us and distracting us with his nonsense talks. He arrived in Dhanbad with the intent of learning and living with us for one whole month. We wanted to join him happily, but after his arrival, we wanted him to go back to his place as soon as possible. He was a pain and a disgusting old man. He irritated both of us with his story had to offer me. I needed to understand that I couldn't trust any stranger with blind-folded eyes. I came to know about all his misdeeds after two months.

Actually, whenever Sahil and I went out of that room for whatever reason, we left our laptop with him. We were unaware of the fact that all our contents, details about our works, personal chats with professionals, and information were at stake. He stole all our content and personal info about our working processes from my laptop. He hacked my Skype account from where I used to chat and plan with the professionals for business work. Even after he had left, we kept the same password for all our social accounts. So, he had access to all my accounts and was using it ruthlessly. I didn't know whether he came with this plan in his head or he decided to victimize us after coming to my place. But whatever happened, it happened for no good reason. I felt really bad, knowing that the person whom I saw as my friend did this to me.

behaviour. He was a very negative person who spread negativity all around and sucked every bit of positive energy from his surroundings. He was too ridiculous to handle. We were pissed off because of him.

Thankfully, after two weeks, he said that he wanted to leave because Dhanbad was too hot to handle and his body wasn't accepting the city's temperature. He couldn't live here anymore. We were blissful when he told us. I am grateful to the hot Sun that summer season for saving me from an evil spirit. The universe helped me get rid of him by heating up my city's temperature that year. We were excited to see him leaving finally, but, of course, we didn't utter any derogatory words to him that could hurt him, since he was our guest. We dropped him off at the railway station and he went away. After that, we kept in touch with him and talked to him occasionally as if I had no remonstrance against him. BUT...He wasn't done yet!

Everything that happens in one's life has its own role to play. The Bangalore guy's story didn't end there because I deserved to face the consequences this

Well, we will talk about the consequences I faced due to his messy appearance in my life later on. Before that, I'd like to relate what happened to me in the midst of my struggling phase.

DEALING WITH RIGHT PERSON AND WRONG PERSON

I started getting loads of work to get through before a deadline. I spent a whole day on the completion of my projects and client's order from the time customers started giving us orders for our services. I was busy with my work. I rarely got time for my family members, I stopped meeting my offline friends I grew up with, and I stepped out of my house once in a week. I remembered I used to work till late night and woke up early in the morning. Then, getting freshen up most probably in 15 minutes and after that, I rushed to work, switching on my laptop. I spent several sleepless nights just working. I used to take short naps of few minutes to relax a bit and get started with my pending work. But I was enjoying my busy schedule too. And why shouldn't I love it? This kind of work actually was interesting. Luckily, my brother was there to help me and make me relatively comfortable with loads of works.

Besides, I along with my mentor Jai Sharma started "DONE FOR YOU" marketing. I started offering a Sales Funnel Service where I'd do all the setup for my clients for Sales Funnel, which we all also called "Done for You Sales Funnel" Service.

Being a professional service provider, we started this business, which was dedicated to all those clients who wanted sales funnel. With "DONE FOR YOU" marketing, we used to provide our customers with the service of creating sales funnel for them. My clients had to do nothing but just bring traffic to their site and build their subscribers list and then they were good to go for making money. This business also acted as a "take off" plan for me. With it, we generated around $15,000 as revenue in the very first week it started. It was an excellent start and gave us a boost.

I was very fond of cars and bikes, but due to the poor financial condition of my home, we had none. As I started earning a good income, I thought of buying our own vehicle. But first, I decided to buy a bike because bikes were more affordable for me at that tenure. I went to showroom and I chose an APACHE RTR 180 ABS. I paid for it in cash. Woooo! I just can't express the feelings I had in words. It was top of the line and my favourite bike at that time. I was so happy buying my favourite bike with my own earned money.

The next day, I called Vicky Sharma, the marketer whom I met in Delhi. I talked and asked for further plans. He informed me that he was coming to Patna on the eve of Raksha-Bandhan. He advised that we meet and talk about it. For that, he invited me to his place in Patna to catch up. I went to Patna and met him. He took me to his home. We discussed things we were dealing with. I told him that I had bought a bike, that peace and comfort were prevailing, and things were now good in my life. He told me that he had started a private limited company in partnership with four members. His company's name was Blisstro

Marketing Private Limited. I was highly impressed, knowing about him and his work. It feels good to see that people around you are also doing great in their lives. He showed his immense interest in doing Fiverr with us. Actually, I was gaining an expertise in Fiverr, and, adding to the flavour, I was a second level seller on Fiverr. So, he wanted us to favour their business with our expertise. I was fine with it, so I agreed to his bidding.

They already had a Fiverr gig but it wasn't generating any positive results for them. They were unable to get sales from there. The problem was that they didn't attempt to process a few things that they were required to do before making any sale. They just created a Fiverr profile and gig and they were expecting sales.

I had a lot of experiences with Fiverr and knew what was important for any customer that can make them give their orders to us and provide us with positive outcomes. Sahil created a Fiverr video gig on my Fiverr account. I made a professional looking gig. In the very first month, our new video gig started giving positive results. Excluding sales funnel revenue, our gig made around $2,000 as profit.

As I said, the Bangalore guy's chapter was still open. He returned and became a thorn in my side. I was doing better each day, but that guy was trying to ridicule my efforts. He was tormented by jealousy. Keeping grudges against us, he started spiteful gossip against me with everyone in his circle, especially with those who knew me and were somehow connected to me and my business. I came to know about this when a mutual friend of ours had a conversation with me. He exposed him in front of me, telling me everything that the old Bangalore man spoke about me. While talking about our businesses ideas, he suddenly mentioned Bangalore guy's name in our conversation. He asked me whether I know him or met him. When I said yes, that he visited us once, he told me the real story. When I heard it from a third party, I tended to ignore it and disbelieve him. But he showed some snapshots of their chat inbox. Then, I realised that I was betrayed by my "so-called-friend."

Our mutual friend was loyal to me and while chatting with me on Skype, he revealed whatever malicious gossip that the old filthy bad-mouthed man said about me to defame me everywhere in his contacts. That old man was calling me a snake who always acted ungrateful towards everyone, even if they helped me with something. He used abusive language against us. He really had been unfaithful to me, and, for that, I felt bad. I felt I had been stabbed in the back for no reason by someone whom I saw as my friend and whom I helped. Betrayal leaves us at a fork in the road but infidelity of any kind can bring about wisdom and invaluable lessons to be learnt for life.

When I found out about this, I gave him a taste of his own medicine. Angrily, I also used few derogatory sentences against that Bangalore guy in my friend's chat inbox. I told our mutual friend how that old man had been with us here throughout his stay, how he emanated bad vibes to his surroundings, and how he was lazy and wasted our precious time. I even revealed this fact that even my brother and I wanted him to leave sooner as he was good for nothing. We also made fun of him and laughed at him. We advised each other to either stay away from him because he wasn't worth of our true bond. I too brushed him off and maintained a safe distance policy with him afterwards because I concluded that he was a man who wasn't good for any relation and selfishly could harm anyone for his own benefit.

A day later, Bangalore guy called me, and we had a fight. He knew everything I wrote in my chat with our mutual friend. He started yelling and putting allegations on me for defaming him in front of his close friend. Whoa! It was like a thief blaming the cop. After few exchanges of arguments and making derogatory comments to each other, I dropped his call.

I was shocked, realizing that he knew everything I said about him. I was unaware that Bangalore guy had my ID, password, and read my messages himself by hacking into my account. I thought our mutual friend must have told him about my hatred towards him.

There must be something brewing between them. Without wasting any time, I called our mutual friend and asked him to tell me the recent conversations between him and the old guy. He said he didn't utter a single word to that man and that he hadn't chatted with him for the last two weeks. I refused to believe him. So, I argued insanely with both of them. We fought badly.

Even they had a fight lately. When I came across their fights, then my mind clicked and I put two and two together. Our mutual friend did nothing that could harm me but that Bangalore guy got to know about our conversation using some other means. But I still wasn't getting a clear picture in my mind of what was going on. I felt he was being vengeful and would surely do something against me.

Even after our fights and all, he continued to insult and belittle me with other online marketers and my contacts. I thought all he could do was make people feel low and disgusted. He neither did anything good in his life nor was he letting others move ahead in their lives. He had lots of problem with everyone in his surroundings who were doing well. I just asked him to go away from my life and to never contact me ever. He kept grudges against me. Still, I was trying harder to ignore him and his negativity completely. I wanted harmony to be in my life. I was focusing on my work positivity to surround me. I never wanted him to come back for any reason.

While I was working on my laptop, I signed into my Skype account. I was going through the messages in my account and found a chat message in which I complained about my services and seemed against my own strategies to a friend of mine, which might lead him to cancel his order with me. I was shocked because I never sent that particular messages I was reading. Fiercely, I asked my brother Sahil about this nonsense. He too responded saying that he knew nothing about it. Within 5 to 10 minutes, we saw that those messages had been removed because I was online during that time. I stayed numb for a while, getting to see an unusual thing happen to my account. We both thought about the matter and linked up everything. We then realized that it must be that old man from Bangalore who did this in order to defame me. I then realized how misunderstandings arose between me and our mutual friends because of Bangalore guy. Bangalore guy was the only culprit and that friend of mine who had let me know about that cheap guy's misdeeds didn't do anything that could harm me. I felt sorry for the fights that I had with that mutual friend for no reason because of that jerk (Bangalore man).

UNEXPECTED SHIT HAPPENS

In October, I got a blackmailing message from the old man of Bangalore. He and one of his friends from United Kingdom were putting me in a really tough spot. He started threatening to hurt me by ruining my image in front of all my clients and leave my business proclivity devastated if I didn't put money where his mouth was. He was using this tactic to frighten me about some unpleasant and menace outcome in order to get me to do what he wanted or else they would sue me for the business world that I had made after working so hard. The thought that somebody was manipulating my clients into believing false stories about me, making clients distrust me, and creating conflicts between us just appalled me. He wanted bribery amount of Rs. 25,000 in order for him to keep his mouth shut. Making a pitfall trap like that was a violation of the trust that I once had on him.

You must be wondering what might be the story behind the scene and that I must have done something that gave him a reason to threaten me. Actually, in August of 2015, this UK guy approached me to create a sales funnel for him. He paid me for his work. He gave me passwords to all of his accounts, even for JVZoo. JVZoo and Warrior Plus are marketing platform for digital products. JVZoo has a huge market place with all sorts of digital products to promote. JVZoo incorporates everything marketers or affiliates need in one convenient place. They make it easy for sellers to promote, list, and sell their products and give affiliate marketers some great digital products to promote. People can launch digital product that could be an e-Book, video course, or software on JVZoo and Warrior Plus.

One can use JVZoo and then not need third party seller tools. To gain JVZoo services, the UK guy had his account there and there was his expensive product that he was to launch.

And when that old man of Bangalore visited us, I shared a secret with him that I had the password and all access to a JVZoo account of a marketer whose software was too expensive to buy. He insisted that I should copy the download links of his expensive and efficient software that cost $297. The software was very productive and highly in demand for marketers. He told me to get it for free by doing so, and we could share it later without spending our income. I refused to do what he was saying. He started persuading me again and again, giving me different reasons to do it. Although I knew it was illegal, under his influence, I copied the download links of that expensive software. I will have remorse all my life for doing that.

Truly it was said, "Beware of the insider, for he can bring down the biggest setup." I was in a boggy situation because of my foolishness. I gave someone a reason to blackmail me and use me for his own benefits. He had grudges against me because I advised my coaching students not to do business with him ever. I showed his true colours to all the marketers who were working with him then and were in my circle too and there were many people who stepped back and started brushing him off after knowing his real side. He was frustrated and wanted to see me destroyed. That's the reason why he brewed these things using that story and making that story play a leading role for my agony. In his message, he declared that in case I don't pay him 25,000 INR, then he would complain against me to that UK guy. He will let him know that I'd stolen his expensive software without his prior consent. He also included that he would include Jai Sharma's name in it too and make sure my upcoming launch brought no good to me. I was the one who was responsible for whatever was happening to me. But, I never wanted to include my mentor's name in any of my wrong doings, about which Jai Sharma himself was totally unaware.

I was scared. My product launch was on my head. I thought that if he made even a single move against me at such a crucial time, then it would have a negative impact on my launch. More than that, I would be left nowhere in the online business world. I would lose credibility. He could have succeeded in making my bad name at my working platform and feel satisfied taking revenge. Even if he posted anything against me on Facebook with a proof, I would have lost everything that I'd earned in two long years working harder each day. All my hard work and effort would have gone in vain within a few seconds. After knowing this, I was sure that no one would ever work with me thereafter. With fear of starting everything again from a fresh start, I was devastated, as it was killing me from the inside. I was restless. I wanted to go back to my past and change that few minutes of my life that led me to this. I wanted to delete that old Bangalore guy from my past. But since there's no use in crying over spilt milk or regretting the past, I thought about planning what to do and what not to do in order to come out of this situation.

I was disturbed and fearful and was in great need of advice. For an unbiased perspective, I called Vicky Sharma for his suggestion. He told me, "You don't deserve to be threatened for such a silly thing, no matter what; you aren't the only one who's responsible for those messes. Bangalore man took the initiative, and if he does anything to harm your reputation, he'll dig his own grave. You can charge a case against him for defamation. If you feel like it's safe for you to resist, I'd suggest that your best option might be to stand your ground and not give in to the threats. No matter what the outcome of the situation is going to be, it's important to realize that someone who would make threats like this is a culprit, not you." So basically, he guided me not to be afraid and stay calm because he's just taking revenge by threatening to extort money from me but he must be a coward to blackmail me using a virtual medium and not confronting me in person.

I was learning the ways to launch online products because I was thinking of getting into launches sooner as well as working on a service project with Jai Sharma. Those blackmailers knew the fact that I was under Jai Sharma. So, they directly contacted Jai Sharma and briefed the whole story telling to him about my mistakes and everything that could turn to be in their favour. Jai Sharma then called me immediately and scolded me for this nuisance. I told him everything exactly the way it happened and asked him for his suggestion. But he got annoyed with the whole story and asked me to pay that blackmailer money. He said that what Vicky advised was often easier said than done. This situation needed to be handled with utmost sensitivity. You should never compromise your safety, integrity, or reputation for some amount of money. Money can be recovered; reputation can't. Just give him the money, settle down the issues with him sooner, and sue this matter at the earliest so that any of our services won't be affected. He also asked me to never repeat such mistake again. I kind of agreed with his opinion and felt that I had no option but to do what that blackmailer was asking.

Without any second thought and delay, I asked that blackmailer to send me the details of his account and transferred 25,000 rupees to him. The next day, I saw his picture on Facebook with his wife. He was having fun at a hill resort with his wife. WHOA! He blackmailed me and got money to rove around a resort with his wife. It seemed like my food had been snatched right from my mouth and he was enjoying it. He neither could work hard nor could earn on his own, so he started blackmailing to make money. I couldn't have thought of such stupidity even in my wildest dream. I was pissed off and annoyed but I kept silent and maintained my calmness. I simply blocked him on Facebook because I never wanted to see his face again in my entire life.

I gave him what he asked for, still, within weeks Bangalore guy complained to the UK guy about my stealing his software. He put all the allegations on me and told the UK guy that I alone stole the software from his JVZoo account. The UK guy immediately called me and yelled at me. He too threatened me saying he would definitely ruin me and my business. I tried to let him know the whole scenario but he refused to listen. He was likely to go to the police. He said that he was going to file an F.I.R against me. Hearing this, I told him that that Bangalore guy was with me while doing this and also involved, but he didn't believe what I said. He said that I was just trying to make an excuse to get rid of this. He was unwilling to accept his Bangalore guy's reality. He was rigid to make a court case against me because I was the one who had his passwords. After that, he hung up on me.

He started texting me on Facebook, Fiverr, etc. He started calling me daily, not just once but 15 to 20 times a day to threaten me. He also wanted 25,000 in rupees from me. Otherwise, he definitely would file an F.I.R. They together took me for an idiot and planned against me. They didn't want me to start my launch, which I had been trying to do for the past few days. They were very jealous, seeing me flourishing. I just couldn't believe what was happening to me. I was too disturbed thinking that if there would be any court cases, it might harm my profession as well as professional reputation. I would be summoned to court and my family would come to know about FIR and complaints against me, which could make them ashamed of me. It was the worst feeling I ever had. I informed Sahil about this. I deactivated my Facebook account for a few weeks and changed my phone number. Then, I got a warning message from them on my Fiverr account, which I never responded to.

Despite giving him (greedy and disgusting Bangalore guy) huge amounts of money from my income, he messed up the entire thing for me. He did everything he could do just to create problem for me. Unfortunately, my way of dealing with threats earlier like that was of no profit. Giving in to threats usually doesn't make blackmailers stop. He and his partner in crime (the UK guy) again planned and messaged me to send them Rs. 25,000 once more. There was no use in transferring such a large amount of my earnings to him. They took me as a kid who knew nothing and whom they could target to get money for a living. They must have had a thought that they can fool me every time and use me by asking for money again and again and by doing this, taking revenge against me. But now, I wasn't at all in the mood to get used in such a lame matter. I decided that I wouldn't give them a single penny no matter what.

Barking dogs seldom bite. One month passed by and they did nothing. Finally, I won suing them off from my

FINALLY, WE GOT STARTED FOR REAL

Our Fiverr video business was booming, its results amazed us and declared that it was there to stay in the market. When we started it, we took help from the tools available on Facebook for getting sales. I used to get all my clients for sales funnel from Facebook. I added all my client whose sales funnels I created to my Facebook's friends list. Yet, the whole format and business idea of sales funnel started fading away from the market.

I met a guy named Finn from abroad. He wanted to launch an Internet marketing information product, and, for that, he wanted my help. *Information product means e-Book or a video course. Whereas, Product Launch means releasing a digital product on a platform* life. I had repentance that I should not have given that Rs. 25,000 (for which I'd worked hard). I thought that was my biggest mistake but, as they say, "all's well that ends well." So the story ended on a better note that they're now out of my life forever without harming me.

like JVZoo or Warrior Plus. I was also in need of a partner who had an online product. He had a product; I had technical knowledge and had already learnt a lot about launches from my own research and from taking classes with Jai Sharma. We were a perfect launch maker at that time. So, I agreed but only on the condition that I would integrate the sales funnel as well as handle all the technical work but he had to create the whole information products on his own.

Finn and I took the initiative to launch. We discussed, planned, and executed. Jai Sharma, my mentor helped me a lot with my first ever product launch. It took us one whole month to get done with all the resources we needed for our launch. One other foreigner was in partnership with Finn and me. His work was to get affiliates who could bring sales for us.

I activated my old Facebook account and wanted to set up a business presence on Facebook. I'd received multiple emails from people, but I didn't want to set up personal accounts for business related purpose or to have my personal presence felt there, so I set up a new Facebook account, a business account.

I launched for the very first time from my new account in January 2016. It was a big HIT. Its result blew me away. This launch was a feather in my cap. Customers were happy. Conversion rate of my sales funnel was good. People in that market started recognising me. Everyone praised us for our work in the launching world. All of them liked everything our launch dealt with, especially the website design. Sahil was the one who designed and built Web pages. His work was of rare quality and one of a kind in that field. He was handling all the designing things like a PRO. I had to admit it as a proud brother that Sahil did a stupendous designing work and worked day and night for our first launch. I must say, he worked much harder than I did for sure.

Absolutely, January 2016 was the most fortunate and best month for me and my brother so far. We generated maximum income that month that exceeded that of all the other months from the very start of our business. I got a good number of clients from my Facebook. Suddenly, my Fiverr sales funnel also started generating revenue for us. An idea that failed once came back to life again. We were seeing a totally different approach to business. We were making great margins and paying ourselves well.

In the next month of February, I again launched another product with Finn. It also became profitable. We both were happy, seeing responses of our colleagues, customers, and other fellow marketers. The results of both the launches boosted our confidence.

Apart from my work, I often talked to Vik Pandey, who was my mentor along with Jai Sharma. They were impressed with my work. He came up with a new idea. He told us about e-Commerce and asked us whether we were free enough to give it a shot as e-Commerce business was booming.

CHAPTER - 4

STEP IN ONLINE BUYING-SELLING WORLD

March 2016

We researched the e-Commerce business after being told of its prospect. E-Com or e-Commerce marketing is the practice of guiding online shoppers to an e-Commerce website and persuading them to buy the products or services online. We kept our spinning wheels to explore more about it. Sahil and I believed that it wasn't that hard and we thought of giving it a try. So, we decided to get going. We called Vik Pandey, keeping the mega vision on our head, and told him we decided to partner with him in his business model for e-Commerce.

Vik Pandey and I jumped right in it to start our own e-Commerce empire. We were excited. To get started with an e-Commerce business model, Vik Pandey got a company registered in the U.S., so that we could begin other proceedings using Shopify. We chose Shopify because it has everything a person needs to launch, run, and manage a successful e-commerce business. Shopify is a complete e-Commerce solution that allows you to set up an online store in which you can sell your goods. It lets you organize your products, customize your storefront, accept credit card payments, track, and respond to orders, all with a few clicks of the mouse.

It's also super easy to use and it requires zero tech skills, so anyone, even newbies, can get an online store and run it promptly. So, Shopify, being the best e-Commerce software for small business, gave us a lot of reasons to use it as our e-Commerce platform.

Beginning with investment and working our way

through checkout, we attempted to try our luck with e-Commerce. We always knew e-Commerce was expensive but anything that you expect to make money is expected to take money too. To understand e-Commerce in a better way, to learn how to set up an e-Commerce store, to gain the knowledge of the effective ways to sell different kinds of products online, and to master it, Vik Pandey invested $2,000 for a group coaching in Facebook. We kept on exploring and trying more and more ideas with our planned model. However, we didn't get any single sale for any of the items we were selling. It wasn't nearly as simple as we had imagined.

April 2016

I was working on Shopify and besides, I was into launching too. After a lot of planning and discussing of ideas with the team of Blisstro, (the company that Vicky Sharma opened with his team) together, we launched a software product on Fiverr. That software product was all about giving relevant information about how to make money on Fiverr. My brother and I were already making good money using our models of doing business in Fiverr. Not only this, we were also among the second top sellers there. We knew exactly what it took to reach your goal on Fiverr and how to land your feet among top sellers. Our Fiverr products began to reach out to a great number of clients to explain the awesome simplicity of our information product. Our launch was successful. We got good reviews for our product. Our Fiverr product clinched the title of 'product of the day' and we became top seller for that information product. It generated huge revenue for us. I was earning quite massively with launches and from the LISTS I had. Both fields were boosting our finances.

On the other hand, I was still a learner on Shopify. We struggled through. My brother and I kept on researching more about marketing ideas. We tried following some strategies and training tips for selling products online using Shopify. We browsed through Ali Express and eBay, picked up few products and tested on them to know whether or not anyone would buy it from us. We created an advertisement to run a Facebook Ad. This Facebook Ad did help us. We got our first sale. We got an order for a necklace that had been picked from Ali Express, the Chinese e-tailing giant that's listed on the NASDAQ. This model of running e-Commerce is known as drop-shipping. We were very happy. Overly excitedly, we did another ad on Facebook and were expecting sale after sale using same strategy. But, to our great surprise, it turned out to be a massive black hole. After one sale, we got none and that was upsetting for the three of us.

Regardless, we carried on. I realized that in e-

Commerce, one requires a lot of hit & miss to get things right, and that's why we needed patience. Moreover, if you try to test anything, you're likely to deal with errors. No one achieved their goal without facing problems and making errors while they were processing initially. I tested many items, not stopping even once until and unless I started seeing good results. We tested lots of items using Facebook Ads. We spent a lot of expenses on Facebook Ads but none were meeting our expectation and were producing negative ROIs (return on investment). The income from sales we were getting was far less than what we were spending.

Vik Pandey was funding this whole thing. He was investing a lot of money like crazy, but to no use. It was April now, and we were facing losses after losses while starting e-Commerce. Sometimes, even if you work hard, you encounter a bit of an immovable problem. It was awful. We had already wasted loads of money and weren't seeing any good results. I was thinking negatively about our efforts and survival here in this market, but we trusted each other and we knew that "that day" would come soon when we would crack the code. Vik Pandey and I had a 50-50 split in ownership and were 50% shareholders each in e-Commerce, but since I alone couldn't afford that massive investment that was required for our e-Commerce, he was helping us initially by funding himself and not bothering us.

My brother was very hard working and was labouring really hard on Shopify. He was learning Facebook Ads in a regular way and continued it until he understood the real strategy to running and monitoring ads perfectly. On my part, I kept on launching products with some of my Facebook friends in order to earn some extra money for us. Launches never were stable business. I knew I couldn't depend wholly on launches for getting stability because when you launch, you just make money with your product and you build lists. It's obvious that your list stop responding after a certain length of time. This was why we never depended on launches but still kept it as an option to making money at a time of need.

E-COMMERCE TALKS

May 2016

I saw that there were a number of business personalities who became successful with e-Commerce. I read so many testimonials and saw live videos relating to their success stories whenever I browsed through my Facebook account. People there narrated their whole journey, giving a full description of how they started and how far they've come. Their success stories always motivated me to persevere in e-Commerce despite the failures and inspired me to do better. My brother and I were competitive always and thought that if they could do it, then why couldn't we do it? We could also flourish with e-Commerce if we gave in our best shot.

We never let any of those business planners make us feel intimidated. We never thought of us being inferior or timid in front of them. We always saw ourselves being better than they were because they were at that level after 30 or even 40 years of their life but my brother and I had just 16 and 18 years of experiences with life respectively. We always had our positive points in our heads to keep us moving ahead on our way. As we were tech savvy, we knew a lot about online and Internet marketing and all other different online data and subjects. We had always been confident that we surely would be successful someday, sooner or later.

Our group coaching wasn't benefiting us after a certain point in time. At the initial phase, our mentors helped us on Facebook, but immediately after getting payment from us, they started keeping us waiting for their replies. They asked us to email them the question to which they replied back with answers according to their convenience, preferably after 24 hours. Waiting a long time to get answers to our questions and solutions for our problems was frustrating us. I was angry & disappointed with their services.

I wasn't getting anything to overcome the problems we were facing, so I prayed. I started praying a lot each day. I always prayed to God and Goddess for giving me success in our e-Commerce business. I didn't eat in the morning until after I had prayed for half an hour. Thinking God would take me to where I want to be, I did whatever I could to make my God happy.

June 2016

Nothing was working for us. Vik Pandey and I decided to get a better coach because group coaching was a total waste of money and effort. It wasn't offering us any valuable knowledge and was of no use to our business model at all. Whereas, a personal mentor would help their students to get things done efficiently, one on one. Personal mentors are also likely to give tips and share some effective tricks and techniques to sell an item online. This was the last straw for us.

We hired a personal mentor for e-Commerce to meet our goals. He was a millionaire and also had a few successful students in this genre. He was willing to guide us very well. He charged $10,000 as his coaching fees. This was a big investment to make but, somehow, Vik Pandey managed to pay that amount. Now, we were heading on the right path. I must say that getting him as our mentor at the right time was a boon for us. We were happy with the decisions that we had made lately. I started making calls with my mentor for hours to get training from him. The coaching module involved a 1-2-hour Skype call every week.

Our mentor saw us as beginners at first. But when I showed him my websites, he became really impressed with our work. Sahil was a website designer earlier and had a lot of experience in it, so it was very obvious that our websites were impressive and looked really good. He complimented our website designs, which were simple yet highly professional. There were some menus in our websites that he liked very much and applauded. He told us that he liked this idea and surely would have to implement this feature on his own website too. I was very happy hearing the praise and nice words about our work from such a big star of online world himself. He said that he would try our ideas that we implemented on our websites and that took me to the cloud 9. I also told him about the products that we launched and sold online earlier.

Then, he realized that we actually weren't beginners but already knew a lot of things about the online world. After I expressed my views and after he came to know about my accomplishments, he understood that actually I just needed his help with Facebook Ads. Setting up e-Commerce was tough in India, but he knew all of that. We discussed the different problems we faced while starting such as PayPal issues. He said he could relate to me, as he was from Nigeria and settled in UK. He also faced a problem while dealing with it then. We started making our bond stronger after a few conversations with each other after every call. He never asked me to ask questions only by email or Skyping. He was ready to guide me even in Facebook chats. He presented himself to be a real guide who never ran away from his responsibility of being a mentor and always gave us an ideology to follow the right direction. He never delayed in giving replies to questions and never kept us waiting for any solution, unlike what the group coaching members did. The moment I dropped a message to question him regarding anything related to ads, he gave me a quick response immediately on the spot. We were happy with the service that he was providing. He was a real preacher to be followed.

He guided me on how to scale and monitor Facebook Ads. My brother and I were learning every aspect of Facebook marketing from him. He showed me how to monetize. He gave me all the briefs on how he worked and maintained his sheets. He taught me ways to kill bad campaigns and to calculate profits and loss. He guided me on everything relating to Facebook Ads. Basically, my mentor helped me in scaling up my ideas and e-Commerce business. We were fortunate enough to get under his guidance at the right point of time. I turned 18 in the month of June 2016.

YO! GOT A POTENTIAL MARKET

July 2016

Things started getting better by now. We picked up a winner product because the former products that we selected were high in demand. We finally cracked the code and our strategies worked out. After a while, our e-Commerce business got to the peak. Our e-Commerce models started flourishing and we were now into gaining profits. Anyway, it all came to head about five months later.

We were indebted to my partner for more than $25k. Vik Pandey was financing everything and he invested that huge amount on us to try our hands in this and to begin our e-Commerce journey. We started paying off our debts to our partner Vik. My mentor, Maine, and I were continuously in touch. Whenever I had any doubt, I used to call him for his suggestions, sometimes twice a week. We slowly became very good friends. He was quite impressed with my sales funnel when I showed it to him. He also praised the model that I was using for up-sell and the way I was monetizing my customers. My brother started to call him. He set up the entire thing the same way for him as well but he missed few things in his sales funnel that could have helped him to get more sales. But we did it for him. We told him earlier that we were sales funnel creators as well, so we had a strong sales funnel in the market.

We cleared all the debts that we had in the month of July. I paid off our partner all the expenditure that he invested that led us on the road to e-Commerce. That July was just phenomenal for growing our business. We made over $85,668. OH MY GOD! We drastically improved our business ideology and marketing model. From $12,000 in June to $85,668.94 in July was beyond our expectations. It was a high jump for us. Our journey was full of excitement, implementing a plethora of ideas. I never thought we could earn this much but we did it. An intermediate exam failure was about to achieve success in his business and real life.

Since lots of orders were being placed, we needed to fulfil our customers' orders on time, sending our customers the tracking numbers, emailing them, giving relevant information about their ordered product and we also had to focus on some new products. It was getting harder to manage and we were in need of outsourcing these so that we could scale up our game. The biggest fight for me was handling the initial transition. After that, we had loads of work, so I hired two of my friends to work for us on a salary basis. I told them that they would get a payment of 10,000 INR on the last day of each month. They were good friends of mine whom I've known from childhood. My family knew both of them very well. They agreed to help us in our work. They started coming to our house daily to work. Now, two more new members were added to my team.

When I informed them about my work, my friends

were shocked that we had reached the point of earning what no other government employees earn and at an early age of 18. They just couldn't believe their eyes and ears. They weren't jealous of me. Instead, they were happy seeing me achieve my dreams because they knew my family's financial condition. They were astonished at the change of our life and were amazed that we planned a career that was so exciting. They asked me to tell them everything in detail. I told them the whole story, describing how it all started, what I went through and how I struggled.

It was a very busy month. I didn't step out from my house for weeks, except to go to the GYM in the morning. The whole team was busy delivering our customers with better services. We worked together till late at night for several months.

CHAPTER - 5

FROM GRIEF TO GLORY

August 2016 brought to me the biggest earning as compared to previous earning in other months. I crossed over $250,000 this month with e-Commerce business. I along with Sahil, Vik Pandey, and my parents were so happy with our accomplishments. It was mind-boggling. What we achieved that month was a milestone for us. I was also planning to launch a product next month with Jai Sharma and a few other partners. That launch was for a software product that was informative and productive in its content. This "Smart Ads Builder" has been playing an important role for the users to run their Facebook Ads without any hassle and soon see results for sure after following it. Smart Ads Builder is a smart web-based software that provides a complete solution that puts all the pieces together to help a user build a successful ad campaign for driving leads and sales. It's powerful because of its features that set it apart. It can help in writing high performance ad content for user as it automatically builds a new buyer audience to target a user's new ad and it spies on the latest trends and use them to get more leads for the user's business.

We had surety that this product launch would generate positive outcomes and good feedback, so we were working harder to make it happen. In September, we finally launched the product that we worked hard on for weeks and expected that launching to hit the market with a bang. Indeed, that launch was a huge success. The turnover from the launch was on a big scale, approximately $251,000 within a week. My partners and I were joyful and very satisfied about the revenues we made with the launch.

Now, in the month of October, my brother and I came up with a new idea. We already possessed competence and had a good idea about how to sell things online. So, Sahil and I thought about starting a new Shopify store. We were absolutely ecstatic about our new baby. Our team doubled in size in a couple of months.

We, together with our team, worked hard on that project and crossed the margin of $400,000 in a single month from that new e-Commerce site. Overall, I reached a total earning of over $660,000 from both of my stores, and when Sahil calculated the revenue we got as a perk in the last two months, we found that it was $251,000 from the launch, $240,000 from my e-Commerce in the last month, and $660,000 from my e-Commerce revenue in the latest month as well. In total, we made over $1,000,000 just in two consecutive months. I just don't know exactly where I was that time, either on top of this world or in another world. I had a superb feeling. OMG! I just can't wrap my feeling even if I use millions of words to describe it. I was on cloud 9. Our planet must be moving the way we wanted it to. It was the greatest achievement for us till date. I thanked the almighty GOD, the compassionate, the merciful, for his endless blessings, who kindly helped me for making it happen. We never thought or dreamt of touching that big figure within couple of months. Those were wonderful months for my family, my team, and I.

ADVERSITY LED DIVERSITY

Achievements are precious and timeless just like the precious happiness of family. And what better way to celebrate milestones in your life than bringing smiles on the faces of your family members? So, we planned to purchase a car on Dhanteras (Dhanteras is an auspicious occasion celebrated in two days before the festival of lights, Diwali). My brother and I decided to buy an XUV 500. It was a captivating car that has bold new styling and was filled with exciting new technology. That car was mid-sized, so that all my family members could fit inside. My parents and all members in my joint family were so happy and super excited. It feels great when you're the reason that smile is on your family members' faces. You feel satisfied and contented from within. Their happiness is worth all your labour and struggles that you've been through.

While we started seeing alienation coming from our neighbours, all of a sudden, their reactions changed towards us. Their reactions and energies were too negative. As it's tough to live a positive life around negative people, my mother didn't find it comfortable to stay in that neighbourhood anymore. She remarked that good energy is contagious but bad energy is infectious. Negative energy paralyzes your thoughts and actions. It adheres to you and can flow after you. We had enough money to buy a new flat by then, so why take the risk? That's why we decided to move somewhere else.

We're now living in a new place. Now, we're in a good, positive environment where our neighbours don't bother us much, where everyone living in our surroundings has a good aura and are busy with their own lives, where they mind their own business until and unless you ask them to interfere. Even today when I thought about our former house, I got tears in my eyes. Only I and my family know how we lived there, how we fought for our survival with collapsed ceilings and holes in doors and windows during rainy season, and how eight of us managed to adjust at nights to sleep in only two rooms.

I was emotionally attached to that place and, the night we left, I cried like a baby and didn't want to leave that place where I'd lived for almost 18 years, started a business that led me reach here, where my team grew, and where I'd seen my life taking a U-turn. So, we didn't abandon that place completely. My mom and dad usually kept on visiting there once or twice a week.

Another month came up to fulfil another desire. In November 2016, we bought our own Villa and a Bungalow, both in a developed and yet growing area, to experience a better quality of life in a top-notch society of Dhanbad. The Villa that I booked had my name on it and was actually under construction. The sooner it gets completed, the sooner I will move in.

This month also, our e-Commerce boomed a lot.

Christmas day got a lot of clients to get through our website doors. People excitedly participated and placed a lot of orders for a lot of items. Christmas is fast approaching and so does sales on such festivity increases rapidly as people opted for shopping various products either for themselves or for the purpose of gifting it to their loved ones. As a business owner, it's necessary to be constantly on the lookout for new profit-making opportunities. So, we tried marketing strategy on different shopping websites with an objective to enhance sales during that festive season. Our e-Commerce business got more profitable this month due to Christmas.

I wish to thank all my team members behind the success of our e-Commerce stores for getting everything done right on time and for delivering better customer services to all clients whether they buy item for $1 or for $10,000. All our customers were and are equal to us. Customer support is an essential but yet tiring and time-consuming aspect of running any business. In today's world more than ever, it's very important to provide great customer support. Our team thought about customer support in a whole new way. We worked together as professional team to manage our customer support and turn each customer into ambassadors for the products we were selling and for the services we were providing. I wanted my customers to generate word of mouth referrals and give positive feedback of our services and products because they had a great customer-support experience. The only way to achieve this goal of ours was to provide the best possible support we could give to each customer. We've managed our own busy help desk efficiently and have strived to keep our own customers happy and I hope that my whole team and I continued to work that way. We are continuously refining our own procedures through the lessons we learn by dealing with our customers every passing day. Whenever we sold something, we always kept our eyes on our customer's satisfaction. We've had a dedicated staff to support our customer's rights and to resolve their queries about any product.

Life became good and exciting. Now, I'm happy with my life. In December 2016, I calculated the earnings that I made the whole year. The total revenue was $2,000,000. Beyond my expectation, *I was earning exactly the same amount of figures that I once dreamt of.* It was an excellent feeling to earn such a BIG number. A year before, I always admired the entrepreneurs whose success stories I read, and they earned exactly what I started earning a year later. *Dreams do come true.* You should just have the courage to dream and take a step towards making your dream come true. I dared to dream and, finally, I was at the stage where I was getting everything that I was supposed to have and desired. I was fortunate enough that I got on the right path just at the age of 18. Some people's success comes at 30 and for a few, it comes at 50, but success really comes your way if you want it desperately by working for it. You just need to have your focus on that particular area while ignoring what others say about you behind your back.

When I told my parents about my earnings, they couldn't believe the numbers. They all gave me a warm hug. Once again, I thank God for making this happen. I also purchased a new car, SWIFT DEZIRE and gifted it to my uncle as a tribute to thank him for whatever he did for us.

I stopped selling for a week, took a break from my busy schedule, and went on a pilgrimage to visiting some temples with my whole family in my own car in January. It was really fun spending time with my family and taking them for a vacation where I was funding every expense. I enjoyed this with my family to the fullest because I knew that I wouldn't be able to spend quality time with them later. So, in the beginning days of 2017, we visited temples and took blessings from sacred places.

After coming back from our vacation, I purchased a new bike a KTM RC 200. In 2013, I desired buying a Duke or RC 200, or any other KTM bikes. It took four years, but it happened. I feel lucky each time I get something I desired one after the other. Last year's six months and the starting of this year had been amazingly successful for me. I'm sure that more of my accomplishments are on their way. It's just the beginning for me. The whole picture is yet to be seen and lived.

FINAL WORDS

You may not be born with a silver spoon in your mouth, but in your hand lies a tool to carve out for yourself a golden one. No one should ever give up on their dreams. According to a Japanese concept, if others can do it, you can too. If no one did it, then you must do it so you go down in history as the first one to do it. You should never look down on yourself. Sometimes, it might seem as if the situation is totally adverse and things aren't taking shape the way you expected. Just keep going on and on without taking any pause. Even if it seems that GOD is coming too late, have faith and believe that he's indeed planning to come in a way bigger than you can imagine. Be focused on where you're heading. Be patient and never lose hope.

Just decide what you want to do in your life and don't

settle for anything less. If you can't dream of becoming the sun, then you should dream to become a star at least. Just make sure of one thing: that you become something better than good. Think outside of the box. Think about being in that 1% of people who achieve success, and not to be counted among that 99% of people who just dream about an amazing life but never work to achieve their dream. My dear reader, don't lose hope after failure. I've been there and I know how it feels. Believe that you can live your dream. Do remember that success always starts with failure. Just keep moving forward to pursue your dream.

Always think that you're a champion. All improvements in your life begin with an improvement in your MENTAL PICTURE. Make sure you feel, "I'm awesome." Make sure you feel "I can do it." Make sure you feel "I can be successful." Make sure you feel "I can truly live a wonderful life." Make sure you feel "I can break the record." Make sure you feel "I'm born to do something better than everyone." Make sure you feel "I too can be there." Yes, never be overconfident but always keep your confidence high.

Ensure that you set goals and achieve what you believe because if you're confused like I once was and have no idea where to go, a burning passion to achieve your goal will see you through. If I could do it, then, trust me, you would NAIL it if you give it a shot. At least, take one step toward you goal: write it down. I want to tell all my readers that the only thing you cannot do is what you haven't attempted to do. If you're going to dare to aim for it, surely you'll do it.

I extend all my best wishes to each one working out there with a dream in their eyes. GOOD LUCK!

www.ingramcontent.com/pod-product-compliance
Lightning Source LLC
Chambersburg PA
CBHW030750180526
45163CB00003B/970